DECONSTRUCTION
OF PSYCHOTHERAPY

DECONSTRUCTION
OF PSYCHOTHERAPY

T. Byram Karasu, M.D.

JASON ARONSON INC.
Northvale, New Jersey
London

This book was set in 12 point Bookman by TechType of Ramsey, New Jersey, and printed and bound by Book-mart Press of North Bergen, New Jersey.

Library of Congress Cataloging-in-Publication Data

Karasu, Toksoz B.
    Deconstruction of psychotherapy / T. Byram Karasu.
       p. cm.
    Includes bibliographical references and index.
    ISBN 1-56821-821-4 (hc)
    1. Psychotherapy—Philosophy. 2. Deconstruction. I. Title.
    [DNLM: 1. Psychotherapy. 2. Psychological Theory. WM 420
K178d   1996]
RC437.5.K37   1996
616.89′14′01—dc20
DNLM/DLC
for Library of Congress   96-12693

Manufactured in the United States of America. Jason Aronson Inc. offers books and cassettes. For information and catalog write to Jason Aronson Inc., 230 Livingston Street, Northvale, New Jersey 07647.

CONTENTS

PREFACE

Let me begin with the observation that the word *deconstruction* has not yet found its way into common parlance, nor has it introduced itself into the language of psychotherapy per se. It is gradually gaining ground, however, as a post-modern concept that posits a critical way of thinking—*the breaking down of form to find new meaning.* More specifically, it constitutes an oxymoron that combines the two contrasting concepts *destruction* and *construction*, both of which, of course, have been with us for a long time. As a more recent variation of such terminology, the rubric *deconstruction* may also be applied in any arena and can be analogized to the processes of disassembling and reassembling even the most solid structures.

In the restoration or renovation of a house, for example, the following familiar scenarios often occur: many may choose to live in an already erected edifice that is presumably tried and true, and can even outlast the space they inhabit; when the place in which they are comfortably settled and to which they have become ardently attached has outlived its use-fulness, they are, alas, reluctant to depart. Others choose to repair the worst of the damage and may or may not resurrect the rest, and yet others would rather reject whatever still stands and begin totally anew. Somewhere in between are the deconstructionists, who elect not to destroy what already has been built, but to carefully reexamine existing elements. This is an integral part of the search for new shapes and structures without necessarily negating those of the past, paving the way for unprecedented possibilities that better befit contemporary needs. In short, deconstruction is the antithesis of a rigid or reified foundation of ideas. Instead it reflects an open outlook or vision, at the same time subjecting to scrutiny the very construction that one seeks to change.

In the deconstruction of psychotherapy, the first issue is the functions and failings of theoretical foundations, and most critically for the clinician, the gap between theory and practice.

I am concerned here with the purposes and perils of ardent allegiances to theories, irrespective of the advantages or disadvantages of a particular school or strategy. This means examining the many uses and abuses of the clinician's belief system, for him as well as for the patient. Whereas the therapist naturally needs to have a body of beliefs to which he can be professionally committed, inability to look beyond them can be countertherapeutic as well; hiding behind one's theory may be as problematic as not having one to relinquish. Moreover, deconstruction of the positive and negative elements of theory reveals their fated fragility, as they must forever straddle an unsettled status that resides somewhere between myth and truth.

Second, with the deconstruction of a plethora of psychotherapy schools, I discovered that the field was pervaded by three predominant paradigms, a "therapeutic troika" of dynamic, behavioral, and experiential approaches. In fact, they had originally followed a chronological course within the cultural contexts of their respective times. At the turn of the century, Freud's psychoanalysis and other dynamic therapies came out of, and in answer to, an age of sexual repression that viewed the psychopathology of its day in terms of unconscious libidinal conflicts that needed to be brought to the surface if man was ever to be cured of his psychological ills. Subsequently, with the mid-twentieth century rapid rise of technology and the impending replacement of man by the machine, an age of anxiety arose, which behavioral therapies attempted to address by systematically desensitizing man to his environmentally derived anxieties and reconditioning him to relaxation responses. Lastly, in the latter part of this century, with the wholesale subordination to outside forces larger than himself, man was unwittingly ushered into an age of alienation in which he felt diminished and alone, if indeed he hadn't totally lost touch with himself and his feelings; in keeping with these concerns, experiential therapies sprang up to fill this particular void. Here the deconstruction of psychotherapy revealed that these divergent and often competing orientations nonetheless can become complementary modalities in the totality of treatment.

Third, an exploration of the unresolved question of what produces change or cure in psychotherapy resulted in a disassembling of the specificity versus nonspecificity controversy, a dualistic dilemma concerning the way therapy is presumed to work. In examining the elements of this conflict, it was discovered that there are alternative meanings to each of these terms. Very briefly, three different versions could be construed from a deconstruction of this dilemma: (1) sectarianism versus eclecticism, which refers to therapeutic effectiveness through the exclusionary use of one approach for all psychological ailments, in contrast to a multimodal orientation; (2) individuality versus universality, which upholds that a particular school or strategy is good for a particular problem, as opposed to belief in the salience of common core ingredients as the crux of therapeutic cure; and (3) techniques versus relationship, which differentially recognizes as secondary versus primary the role of the human interpersonal encounter in relation to specific strategies. Collectively, these provide a closer and more subtle look at the spectrum of thinking about how psychotherapy heals.

Fourth is the deconstruction of psychotherapy research and the scientific schema that is utilized to evaluate its effects. At bottom, this chapter asks the perennial question of whether psychotherapy can be considered a science or an art. In this behalf, it examines a variety of research and methodological issues, including problems of design and sample selection, statistical strategies, assessments of outcome and process, and of contemporary concern, cost effectiveness and cost benefit. This chapter concludes, at least tentatively, that perhaps psychotherapy is really an art precariously perched on the pedestal of science.

Finally, the deconstructive tables are turned

to a *reconstruction* that attempts to locate universal agents of change amidst the morass of conceptual schemas. Here, three enduring elements—affective experiencing, cognitive mastery, and behavioral regulation—are traced from the dawn of time to recent treatment, and as their respective roles are reviewed in relation to one another, the prospects for synthesis are raised. In the final analysis, their collective applications augur well for the future of psychotherapy as an era of entente is entered.

In the concluding chapter, my epilogue, I envision the end of theory. Yet all is not lost—or won. I foresee future therapists still struggling to be set free from the never-never land of theory, while reductively clinging to the pseudocomfort of their respective gurus. On this unsettling note, I deconstructively contemplate our finite fate—while wondering who will be the "last therapist."

T. Byram Karasu

1

THE CONCEPT OF DECONSTRUCTION

To know is to dissect.
Jacques Derrida, *The Ear of the Other*

Deconstruction is a theory, or critical move-ment, that delves into the structure of history, questioning established assumptions and chal-lenging the foundations of even the most ac-cepted and time-honored concepts. It attempts to do so by breaking down formulated frame-works into constituent parts, with the express purposes of unearthing and undoing en-trenched doctrines and the presumptions that underlie them. In a concerted effort to guard against the suppressive assumption that events of the world can be known with absolute certainty, its modus operandi is to carefully disassemble all rigid or reified belief systems. It is thereby a doctrine that desanctifies—destabilizing secure models erected from seemingly solid, valid, and reliable relations. On a more philosophical level, deconstruction addresses the impossibility of devising any theory or method of inquiry that infinitely answers the complex questions of man. As Stephens (1994) put it, "It confronts us with the limits of what it is *possible* for human thought to accomplish" (p. 22).

As a linguistically bifurcated term that contains contrasting components from two different prefixes—*de* = down or away from, *con* = with or towards—*decon*struction is poised between the purely positive concept of construction (i.e., building or joining together) and the purely negative concept of destruction (i.e., ruining or tearing apart). It simultaneously borrows from both, but it is neither. With its increasing appearance in contemporary vocabulary, the nuances of this term are said to include the notions of contradiction, negation, and cancellation as well as those of feeling challenged, perplexed, and disconcerted (Lehman 1991). At the same time, in order to wrest oneself from the discomfort that these feelings evoke, there occur the accompanying needs to confront the challenge, to grasp what is confusing, and to utilize one's unsettled state as a creative road to new truth. In short, deconstructing can have connotations that are both disarming and liberating as it aims "to expose and unmask, to demystify and dismantle" (p. 25). Moreover, while deconstruction constitutes a form of analysis that accepts no stable reference, perhaps more importantly it embodies such instability as a *necessary precursor to* knowledge and change.

Begun in the 1960s in France by the Algerian-born Zen master of Western philosophy, Jacques Derrida, deconstruction as a theory was originally applied to textual analysis, especially with regard to the ability (or inability) of language to represent reality. Since then, deconstruction as a mode of criticism has been expanded from the reading of literary discourse to many other fields, such as art, philosophy, or architecture, and even to a country or culture. To deconstruct a "text" can now mean to take apart *any* work or existing event, from the Bill of Rights or *The Communist Manifesto* to a Rembrandt painting or Beethoven sonata—to the prescribed tenets of classical psychoanalysis or other non-Freudian schools of psychotherapy. Nonetheless, the method is the same no matter what the subject is: "to strip them of the ideological vested interests in which they came packaged" (Felperin 1985, p. 19).

Deconstruction has other paradoxical properties: It can be viewed as a process of *domestication* (Felperin 1985, p. 218) insofar as it serves to tame wild theories; at the same time, it is a process of de-domestication that functions to disturb institutional as well as individual complacency, to undermine monistic thinking, and to evoke increased indeterminacy. At bottom, it puts everything in question, in effect wiping the slate clean. Simultaneously, taken to its logical limit, it also augurs well for new beginnings. Posed in terms of the self, it both profoundly unsettles us to the core—and thereby *opens* our vision—to newly reveal what may have been looked at but not been *seen* before.

Nonetheless, loosened from familiar moorings, one can easily see the potential threat of deconstruction, as it carries with it the power to provoke formidable reactions from originators and followers in every corner of their well- or ill-constructed belief systems. For example, not surprisingly, the concept of deconstruction has been hoist on its own petard, sweepingly rejected as apocalyptic irrationalism, critical terrorism, and dogmatic skepticism (Lehman 1991); with the addition of irony, it is also understood, paradoxically, as systematic misunderstanding (Felperin 1985).

Let's look at some of these accusations. It is

true that deconstruction always exists *in alio*, by inhibiting the discourse of others, never *in se*, as something present in itself (Lehman 1991), but the search for truth, even what may appear to be excessive truth, is ideally built into any critical system—or at least should be. Although deconstruction seemingly works through the rhetoric of negation, or even annihilation, by emphasizing that "all readings are misreadings" (Evans 1991, p. 177), at the same time it inherently defends itself by self-accusation. The term deconstruction, after all, has the same root meaning as "analysis," to loosen or break up, in order to separate the whole into its constituent parts and to examine a complex entity in terms of its components and their relations.

Moreover, the point should be stressed that deconstruction is not to be confused with destructive criticism; indeed, the connection between them has been viewed as roughly that of a neutron bomb to the hydrogen bomb (Felperin 1985). Thus "both may devastate the texts on which they work—what critical method does not?—but the former, because it leaves all constituent parts undamaged, enables their reassembly . . . in the form of an aftertext that survives the blast. So there may be life after deconstruction after all" (p. 119). In fact, all is not lost; it is simply less familiar.

Thus the ideology of deconstruction is not fatalistic; rather, it provides a rationale or methodology of doubt.

Therefore the deconstructionist is not necessarily a nihilist who upholds the viewpoint that all traditional values and beliefs are unfounded or declares a doctrine that denies any objective ground of truth. However, he or she may be a relativist, an incurable skeptic who is ardently aware of the inherent impermanence of whatever is known. As Evans (1991) has suggested, "deconstruction is not a simple *rejection* of traditional scholarship and rigor: critical, deconstructive reading has to pass through traditional rigor even if the ultimate effect is to show that such rigor is never as absolute and well founded as it claims to be" (p. xv). Furthermore, if deconstruction is to proceed from its own overdetermined center, it has to demonstrate at least relative rhetorical disinterestedness, even though when self-applied the deconstruction of deconstruction may not be able to avoid a certain conceptual duplicity. Self-deconstructing, therefore, must be an active and ongoing *process* that dares to undo itself. Deconstruction procedures have thus been aptly called "sawing off the branch on which one is sitting" (Lehman 1991, p. 61). Without damage to the whole, one cannot articulate it into "pieces" that are (in Husserl's terminology) "independent parts" (Felperin

1985). If you totally dismantled a melody into a collection of sound pieces, you'd miss the song, never mind the singer.

The application of deconstruction to psychotherapy has its own special problems: it suffers from a certain provisional unintelligibility, a lack of neutral critical tools, and, of course, self-deconstructive indeterminacy. To begin with, there is no homogenizing text; instead there are an array of unprecedented heterodoxies in the field with multiple overdetermined centers, and the reification of preferred known concepts to which one holds allegiance, along with their nonneutral languages. Although there is no pure language in any field, psychotherapeutic theories with their dogmatic commitments to particular schools or approaches compound nonneutrality with the logocentricity of their language; there are no truly objective tools either. Just as philosophy cannot start from an absolute uncontaminated beginning, so the conceptual tools that must be used are inevitably implicated in what is to be deconstructed. (See Chapter 5 on "Deconstruction of the Scientific Schema: Problems of Psychotherapy Research.")

As to self-deconstructive uncertainty, it is linked with the idea that there can be no claim to a superior knowledge. The very ideal of a transcendental grounding of knowledge inevitably will turn out to be impossible; Evans

(1991) has aptly pointed out that the idea of ultimate cognitions is no more than another dogmatic committment, itself a metaphysical presupposition. In sum, every theoretical system, however enduring, can be construed as a potential error. As Hegel (1986) put it, ". . . if the fear of error sets up a mistrust of Science, . . . it is not hard to see why we should not turn round and mistrust this very mistrust. Should we not be concerned whether this fear of error is not just the error itself?" (p. 89). Indeed, isn't the ongoing presumption of error the basis of all knowledge?

2

DECONSTRUCTION OF THEORIES: FACTS AND FICTIONS

> If nobody loves theory, it is probably
> because too much is expected of it.
>
> Lawrence Friedman,
> *The Anatomy of Psychotherapy*

The deconstructionist Howard Felperin, who is concerned with the uses and abuses of literary theory, has suggested that in order to be for (or against) any theory, one must "enter into and inhabit" that theory (1985, p. 4). This means to look at the theory not from a safe distance but from the inside out. Doing so is more than a way of gaining intimate knowledge; it is also a method of maintaining a skeptical stance. To really keep an open theoretical mind, one has to maximize, perhaps paradoxically, the very perplexity that one has set out to dispel.

As we attempt here to approach the task of entering into and inhabiting psychotherapy theory, the fundamental question becomes: What do we know about the parameters of theories in general—their functions and limitations, the truths they promise and the myths they perpetuate? Not only may we expect too much of theories, as Friedman suggests, but the converse of his contention is also applicable: if nobody *hates* theory, it is probably because too much is *gained* from it. Theories are thus both overrated and overdetermined. What one gets out of a theory is often more than one is given, and what one hopes to get can be even greater than that.

By definition every theory represents "an ideal or hypothetical set of facts, principles, or circumstances" (Webster's 1989, p. 1223). The inherent nature of theories as tentative constructs metaphorically means an ongoing process of birth, death, and rebirth; it reflects a self-perpetuating and regenerative activity that, by its very nature, makes room for reappraisal (i.e., whereby some part or parts may be rejected while others are left intact), and even replacement (i.e., whereby the entire theory is discarded for an proposed alternative). This innate function and (perhaps) failing of theoretical conceptions—having transitory historical value in keeping with the temper of the times—in turn has direct implications both for the creation—and deconstruction—of theory.

In addition, theories are vulnerable to change insofar as they may be scientifically acceptable, or at least plausible, but can also include unproven assumptions. More specifically, this means that one's theoretical tenets are at best part fact and part fiction. No matter where they fit along the assumptive spectrum, they do nonetheless become frameworks for the organization of data and explanation of events, which operate both to guide one's thinking to begin with and to continually shape and reshape it thereafter. Theories thus steer one's observations by providing direction and focus, forming boundaries for what is included (and thereby necessarily excluded). Because a theory naturally confers constraints, it can force closure upon what one looks at and sees and, in a more extreme sense, consciously or unconsciously suppress information by eliminating whatever appears inconsistent or competitive with preferred preexisting beliefs. In this way theories may reify that which is favored or familiar, and, wittingly or unwittingly, obliterate the unfavored or unfamiliar.

In psychotherapy, such belief systems have been regarded as enduring "myths" (Ehrenwald 1966) or compelling "metaphors" (Spence 1982) that are socially shared and historically sanctioned; they are consensually confirmed but not necessarily based on established fact. A theory can thus function as a kind of transitional object that links the believer to idealized teachers and mentors, thereby providing, in Michels's (1988) thesis, "partially illusory safety and reassurance" (p.11). One's theory of therapy can even subjectively serve as a refuge from reality and personally form an intimate connection to the particular theorist/therapist as a "dwelling for the self" (Wright 1991, p. 329).

It has also been pointed out that theories will never really prevent the occurrence, and possible acceptance, of new observations and hypotheses. Theoretical constructs are by their very nature hypothetical and open, to be potentially proven or disproven, demystified or discarded, in whole or in part. In the above sense, all theory is, according to Rangell (1985), "conjectural, not closed" (p. 60). At bottom, theoretical frameworks can therefore be viewed in two antithetical ways: as doctrinal and as fictional, either inherently self-limited or forever fluid. More likely, theories reside somewhere between the two extremes of scientific reality and illusion.

Moreover, great thinkers have differed in their views of the role of theory in relation to practice. Einstein (1969), for one, exalted the theoretical. He believed that "a theory could be tested by experience, but there is no way from experience to the setting up of a theory" (p. 89). Objective events might be sufficient for a scientist in the research or clinical laboratory, but the theorist could never derive formulations from them alone. The theorist needs the critical ingredient of creative imagination, which refers to the capacity to go beyond the facts, no matter how many are collected. By contrast, Freud (1916–1917), whose elaborate conceptual formulations of the psychic apparatus may have been of equal invention and impact as Einstein's equations, did not agree. Instead he believed that the theory of mind was an afterthought to the relatively direct inferences of the consulting room. More and more therapists are doubtlessly realizing that much of what they learn of psychotherapy ideology, though intellectually intriguing and personally compelling, has limited utility in their daily practice. It may even be counterproductive if the patient is forced to fit falsely into the practitioner's preordained premises.

This discrepancy between the philosophic plane of theory and the pragmatic plane of practice has been validated by comparative research studies of various psychotherapies. These suggest that the therapist's espoused theoretical orientation regarding the nature of the healing process and concept of the ideal therapeutic relationship may not be synchronous with his or her actual applications. In one study that directly examined four reputedly different therapeutic approaches—Freudian, Kleinian, Jungian, and gestalt—to the same patient, descriptive ratings by objective observers failed to differentiate the respective schools of thought (Naftulin et al. 1975). This finding may have come as a surprise not only to the investigators but to the therapists themselves. Subsequently, a review of literature based on several research investigations of this subject concluded: "Effective therapists, irrespective of TO [theoretical orientation], behave similarly . . . for example, they appear confident, express concern, communicate clearly, are empathic, etc." (Sundland 1977, p. 215). It was further discovered that any significant differences in clinicians' technical function had more to do with their general level of experience than with their specific avowed theoretical allegiances.

If the relation of theory to practice is flawed, what then are the benefits—and risks—of learning and accepting a particular psychological theory? Every theory represents "a coherent group of general propositions used as principles of explanation for a class of phenomena" (Random House 1984, p. 1362), such as Newton's theory of gravitation. Theories are usually more or less verified in accounting for known facts or well-established propositions, although their status can still be conjectural. Psychological theories are, more specifically, conceptualizations about the human mind and behavior, which may be especially speculative insofar as they relate to hidden intrapsychic events. Spence (1982), who has been expressly concerned with the scientific and clinical status of the central assumptions of psychoanalysis, uses the word *metaphor* in assessing the theory's truth value (p. 296). He contrasts Freud's archaeological model of the mind as consisting of reconstructions of the past (that is, having "historical" truth) to an aesthetic alternative based on new constructions in the present that in effect create the past (that is, having "narrative" truth). In so doing he highlights the tentative or ambiguous nature of the clinician's interpretive formulations because their historical content cannot be separated from their context in current memory. Thus one's metapsychological premises, like interpretations themselves, are provisional, although they are sometimes treated as fact.

Theories are nonetheless conceptual structures which dually serve to orient one's basic thinking in a particular direction and to guide it thenceforth. Thus theories become anchors by constraining what is believed and what is thereby not believed. Depending upon the fluidity of their boundaries, theories may also offer possibilities for new ideas or for the incorporation of old ideas. For example, it may be easier to add to one's belief system the notion of a collective unconscious (a Jungian concept) if one already believes in the unconscious (a Freudian concept), than to reconcile a behavioral tenet (such as the symptom *is* the neurosis) with a dynamic one (such as the symptom is merely a manifestation of underlying conflict).

Unlike his predecessors, Jerome Frank (Frank and Frank 1991) has not addressed himself to the validity of specific psychological theories or clinical constructs per se, nor to their metaphoric value as temporary conceptualizations or templates that attempt to map reality. Rather, he proposes that the potency of a theory inheres in the belief system's consensuality for the healers. Based on an examination of the cross-cultural function of persuasion and healing, he considers a major theoretical aspect of psychotherapy to be serving to ground the therapist. Psychotherapy accomplishes this by providing a set of guiding principles—a belief system to which the clinician adheres—along with a group of adherents of similar orientation to whom the clinician can turn for professional confirmation and support. A significant implication is that the therapist had best not stand alone in theoretical orientation because he or she gains credibility and confidence through consensual validation.

Equally important, however, is that the conceptual foundation also represents a shared world view between therapist and patient. In the absence of this consensual set of beliefs, the prospects for the patient's compliance as well as eventual change are diminished. This thesis further suggests that like all other theories, which simply set the stage for scientific exploration and typically precede factual validation, psychotherapeutic belief systems are to some extent professional myths. They are compelling and persuasive insofar as they are socially supported, but they have not necessarily been proven.

In fact, theories have a tendency to proliferate to fill the gaps in knowledge. Emotional appeal generally presides until scientific proof can prevail in its place. Spence (1990) has noted that as metaphors become cut off from their referents, they also tend to be reified and become the objects of magical thinking. Instead of remaining provisional, the metaphor itself is transformed into the immutable essence. He suggests:

If the metaphor cannot be falsified by direct contact with its reference, then the way is clear for the metaphor to be taken literally. Instead of one possible account of the stuff of the

mind—a model or hypothesis—the theory in
fashion becomes the final description. The
temptation to accept it as final becomes particularly hard to resist when the metaphor prom-
ises more than it delivers, that is, when it is
couched in language that pretends to refer
when it is merely operating heuristically, or
when it is embedded in a fictional story so
compelling that the reader has suspended all
disbelief. [p. 7]

This brings me from the metaphoric and
consensual value of theories—for the therapist
and patient separately as well as together—to
the tendency of theories to be misused. This is
compounded by the further observation that
theoretical constructs are susceptible to both
socio-cultural and private or internal influences. These can include the prevailing zeit-
geist, the personal history of the theorist, and
the reigning narrative metaphor. The last refers
to the use of language or figures of speech that
may go beyond the data but which gain appeal
and strength from a long tradition of cherished
themes. The metaphor is, in Spence's terms,
what keeps the theory "afloat." According to
this thesis, theories can thus obstruct progress
by interfering with observation and by trap-
ping the believer into testing irrelevant or
inaccurate information. In orthodox psychotherapy the so-called Oedipus complex may be
an example of such a time-honored but some-

times overendowed term. Ever since Freud (1905) extrapolated the famous Greek legend to the guiding principles of psychiatry by claiming that "the Oedipus complex is the nuclear complex of the neuroses . . . which . . . through its after-effects decisively influences the sexuality of the adult" (p. 226), it has attained a level of credence and popularity probably unequaled in the annals of psychological thought.

The greatest peril for therapists is that their most cherished theories are at a high risk of becoming self-fulfilling prophecies. The proposed theory, which is usually consistent with the personalities of its followers, can subjectively alter the perception and collection of clinical data; the alteration forms a feedback loop that returns to the original conceptual formulations. Thus the organizing theory of the observer (what Kuhn [1962] referred to as that person's "paradigm") inevitably influences his or her view of the ensuing events. Adler (1986) illustrates the application of this idea in his exposition of two contrasting orientations toward the psychotherapy of narcissistic personality disorders. In particular he reveals how the respective approaches of Kernberg and Kohut serve to support and validate their own theoretical tenets. In brief, Kernberg's predominant technique of confronting as a defense the patient's grandiose self (as it presumably protects against hatred and envy of the therapist) means that the theoretician-clinician is often the recipient of the very oral aggression that he or she conceptually views as the core of the disorder. In comparison, Kohut's major strategy of allowing the transference to unfold and to become himself the empathic selfobject that was presumably missing in the patient's past (so that he can gradually explore the meaning of the patient's disappointment in the parent/therapist) supports his more benign theoretical contention that such aggression is at most secondary to narcissistic psychopathology.

Adler concludes, "Theory implies a clinical approach that leads to data collection, which tends to confirm the theory and encourage further clinical work, which supports the theory even more" (p. 434). Similarly, Adler believes that the personality of the clinician-theoretician will play a determining role in influencing which aspects of patients will be most likely to be observed and responded to and which will be more easily overlooked (presumably on the basis of the clinician's own unresolved difficulties). In the examples of Kernberg and Kohut, one would expect a difference in the relative degree of aggression and confrontation versus empathy and support each is more likely to apply—and receive—in the clinical situation, as he wittingly or unwittingly tests out his own preferred formulations.

In the final analysis—whether the theory is reverie or reality, proven or unproven—if the therapist relies too heavily on the persuasive power of a particular theory, it will overwhelm his or her thinking as well as constrict approaches to the patient. By so reducing or rigidifying the sphere of working assumptions, he or she is inevitably limited both as therapist and as human being. The patient in turn is also reduced. Levenson (1983) suggests that in the perpetuation of such an attitude, "The danger is that the theory becomes an ideological indoctrination *sui generis* and the patient becomes a disciple" (pp. 89–90).

At the same time, however, therapists must strongly believe in themselves and what they practice, and they must find a method that is most congenial to their personal needs and style. The more passionate a therapist is about his or her theories and personal healing powers, the more likely he or she is to have an impact on patients. One of the enduring ingredients of effective psychotherapy is transmitting one's beliefs, which do not have to be correct—just convincing. Indeed, the therapist's conviction is the basis for "doctrinal compliance" (Ehrenwald 1966) as a major ingredient of all forms of therapy.

Research studies of the efficacy of psychotherapy now confirm that attachment to a
specific school or theoretical orientation may
be necessary for the overall confidence and
professional identity of the clinician. It has
been proven, not merely recommended, that
therapists need to be involved and committed
to a particular point of view. A recent meta-
analysis of outcome studies has scientifically
concluded that "although all therapies are
equally effective, one must choose only one to
learn and practice" (Smith et al. 1980, p. 185).

The complex roles of theories of psychotherapy are therefore often tangled, and at
times tread a thin line between their purposes
and perils. Theory offers the therapist the foundation for personal conviction as well as professional allegiance—to prevent confused
therapists with marginal identities. Theory
serves a mutual and parallel purpose for the
patient: a therapist and therapy to believe and
trust in, at least temporarily. Despite the fact
that each form of therapy may attempt to go
beyond sheer suggestion or persuasion, on
some level such suggestibility is still an essential ingredient of all psychotherapy interventions. The major risks, or abuses, of theoretical
allegiance are those of personal indoctrination
(blind faith as an individual) and partisan polarization (myopia as a member of a particular
group). In either event, the therapist, alone or

among ardent allies, becomes so convinced of the singular correctness of the theory that he or she cannot see beyond it.

But what does the clinician do with these two paradoxical prospects—strongly believing in one's theories, yet not so abiding by them that they erroneously restrict one's therapeutic view? The ability simultaneously to hold and reconcile these opposite perspectives is a quality the effective therapist needs to develop. It encompasses the capacity to accept a basic theoretical orientation while leaving room for alternative possibilities. It also means an understanding of theories in all of their mythic proportions, that is, as legends that endure because they contain collective inspirational value. Whereas such ideologies derive their potency from being rooted and remembered in human social and personal history as they continue to carry to their recipients the ring of truth, they need to be simultaneously seen, with equal fervor, as a form of fiction. Such recognition of the legendary value of theories marks the beginnings of a deconstructive departure from the very tenets to which we are most attached.

3

DECONSTRUCTION OF THE THERAPEUTIC TROIKA: CURRENT OVERARCHING PARADIGMS OF PSYCHOTHERAPY

> A given paradigm merely adumbrates
> new and unforeseen problems which it
> proves, in time, powerless to resolve, and
> for which a new paradigm will have to be
> invented.
>
> Howard Felperin, *Beyond Deconstruction*

Nearly two decades ago Parloff (1975) found more than 140 presumable forms of psychotherapy practiced in modern times; yet the specific ways in which each new modality does or does not differ from its predecessors is still far from clear. In early attempts to schematize the many psychotherapeutic methods and techniques throughout history, Menninger

(1955) and Bromberg (1959) subsumed the various strategies under two dichotomous heads: those which they thought used a principle of suppression in their treatment approach versus those which represented the use of a principle of expression.

Beginning where Menninger and Bromberg left off, Harper's (1959) descriptive overview of thirty-six established Freudian and post-Freudian psychotherapeutic schools, or systems of psychotherapy, attempted to divide the various approaches into two basic categories: those that reflected emotionally oriented or affective forms of treatment versus those that were considered essentially intellectually oriented or cognitive. On a more philosophical plane, Rychlak (1969) addressed the possible implications of ideology for methodology and assessed psychotherapies on the basis of whether they represented therapeutic models that were essentially Lockean (mechanistic) or Kantian (humanistic). Rychlak (1965) also conceptualized psychotherapies according to a comparison of their respective motives: those with a scholarly motive, which are primarily concerned with unraveling the depths of man's nature; those with an ethical motive, which concern themselves primarily with man's self and his values; and those with a curative motive, which directly aim at scientifically derived cure. Offenkrantz and Tobin's (1974) configuration was more implicit. They suggested that all learning (including psychotherapeutic learning) occurs in three modes: by identification, by conditioning, and by insight. Thus one might assume to unite the various psychotherapies on the basis of their primary modes of therapeutic learning, or the major ways in which they presume to effect change in, or cure of, the patient.

As a form of deconstruction, the morass of systems practiced today can be organized according to a therapeutic troika of basic paradigms around which each school may be said to broadly, but distinctively, pivot. These, representing a composite of dimensions, are referred to as "psychodynamic," "behavioral," and "experiential." Each overarching theme represents something of a unity. That is, one's conceptual framework or belief system regarding the nature of man and his ills has a bearing on one's concept of therapeutic modes or curative processes as well as on the nature of the therapeutic relationship between patient and therapist, and ultimately, upon one's methods or techniques of treatment. Although all three paradigms are utilized in the contemporary practice of psychotherapy, each particular paradigm has arisen in reaction to the presumed problems of its predecessors, often unwittingly trading these for others that they themselves, at least potentially, possess.

THE PSYCHODYNAMIC PARADIGM

> There is no exit from the labyrinth
> of interpretation.
>
> Mark C. Taylor,
> *Deconstruction in Context*

Nature of Man and His Ills

The psychodynamic point of view pertains to an appreciation of the complexity of man as victim of turbulent intrapsychic forces with which he continually struggles. Freud (1933) described the major force of this struggle in the origin of the neuroses according to the theory of instinctual conflict: ". . . human beings fall ill of a conflict between the claims of instinctual life and the resistance which arises within them against it" (p. 57). In the orthodox psychoanalytic tradition, man is portrayed as fraught with inner urgings and contradictions, subject to and resisting against a reservoir of impulses largely inaccessible to his conscious self.

The classic dynamic (i.e., analytic) legacy includes the following allegiances: (1) primary concern with the vicissitudes of man's instinctual impulses, their expression and transformation, and, more crucially, their repression, by which is meant the pervasive avoidance of painful feelings or experiences by keeping unpleasant thoughts, wishes, and affect from awareness; (2) belief that such repression is of an essentially sexual nature and that the roots of disturbance reside in faulty libidinal or psychosexual development; (3) belief that these faulty psychosexual developments have their origins in early past and childhood conflicts or traumata, especially those concerning a parental oedipal configuration (i.e., desire for one's opposite-sexed parent); (4) belief in the resilience, persistence, and inaccessibility of oedipal yearnings (i.e., these underlying conflicts remain alive and forever active but out of awareness or unconscious); (5) belief that we are dealing essentially with the psychic struggle and torments of biological man's innate impulses or instincts (id), their derivatives, and the primarily defensive mediation with external reality and one's moral precepts or standards (superego); and (6) adherence to a concept of psychic determinism or causality, according to which mental phenomena (and behaviors) are decidedly not chance occurrences; rather, they are considered to be meaningfully related to events that preceded them, and, unless made conscious, unwittingly subject to repetition.

Change or Curative Processes

In accordance with these tenets, the ultimate task for the therapist, in its most parsimonious and famous form, is to make conscious the unconscious. This means that it is the ongoing therapeutic charge of the therapist to facilitate the emergence and comprehension of unconscious material; the dynamic therapist seeks to undo the repression of the patient and to overcome the latter's natural resistances to this endeavor. The therapist attempts to accomplish this by means of a slow and scrupulous unraveling of the largely historical meanings of mental events and the devious ways in which they may serve to ward off underlying conflicts through defensive camouflage. Understandably, the dynamic goal is thereby a long-range one, perhaps even interminable. At best this concept of cure means opting for total personality reorganization in the final resolution of neurotic conflicts.

The analytical psychotherapeutic systems have consecutively considered as their hallmarks of change the processes of catharsis (following abreaction) and insight. Harper (1959) has broadly defined insight as "the process by which the meaning, significance, pattern, or use of an experience becomes clear—or the understanding which results from this process" (p. 163). He defined catharsis as "the release of tension and anxiety by recounting and/or acting out past experiences" (p. 158). Although both processes have been considered in the psychodynamic tradition, it may be noted that Freud never used the term "insight" per se. The therapeutic process transferred its emphasis from the primary importance of abreaction (catharsis) to the removal of amnesia and the recovery of repressed memories.

According to Hutchinson (1950), there are four successive stages in attaining therapeutic insight: (1) a stage of preparation, which is characterized by frustration, anxiety, a feeling of ineptness, and despair and may be followed by much trial-and-error activity and a falling into habitual patterns or ways of thinking, foreseeing no apparent solution to the problem; (2) a stage of incubation or renunciation, in which one desires to hide or escape from the problem and is resistant to therapeutic or insightful efforts; (3) a stage of inspiration or illumination, in which the whole problem becomes illuminated and solutions suggest themselves (often there is a flood of vivid ideas and a sense of finality accompanied by a conviction of the truth of the insight); and (4) a stage of elaboration and evaluation, in which the validity of the insight is checked against external reality.

Despite the fact that the third stage tends to be most frequently identified with the idea of insight (suggesting an essentially "eureka" or "aha" phenomenon), Ludwig (1966) pointed out that during the typical course of psychotherapy, it is much more common for the patient to experience insight in a drawn-out and emotionally attenuated form.

> The sudden tidal wave of illumination or enlightenment is rare compared to the numerous small ripples of insights which are experienced and intellectually assimilated over a long period of time. Moreover, the therapeutic insights tend to be circumscribed and specific to certain problem areas than the profound and general eureka experiences, such as those described to occur during religious conversion or revelation in which the "whole truth" suddenly is revealed. [p. 315]

In terms of the therapeutic value of the process of insight, Ludwig noted that "there is no necessary relationship between the truth or falseness of insight and therapeutic results" (p. 313). In addition, since intellectual insight alone is felt to be of minimal value, attempts have been made to distinguish between intellectual and emotional insight. However, it is difficult to validate such a distinction (Richfield 1963). Nonetheless Ludwig (1966) hypothesized that insight is therapeutic when it meets all of the following specifications: (1) consistency: the deductions based on the original insight are stable and logically sound regardless of the truth or falsity of the particular content of the insight; (2) continuity: insights must take place within some existing theoretical framework or stream of tradition in which the insight can be tested; (3) personal consequences: the insight must be judged by the fruit it bears in terms of the ultimate use to which the insight is put; and (4) social consequences: the acquisition of insight should allow the person to interact with others in a more honest and meaningful manner.

For some, the questioned role of insight represents a limitation of the dynamic paradigm. While other analysts have had confidence in the role of insight as a therapeutic agent, doubt has been cast on the "insight leads to change" dictum. Schonbar (1965), for example, observed both that not all change is attributable to insight and that not all insight leads to change. However, the fact that insight, even as the ultimate agent of change, does not occur in isolation raises another major consideration of the analytic therapies, that is, that intricately embedded in the psychodynamic curative process is the critical role of the therapeutic relationship.

Nature of the Therapeutic Relationship

The deliberate and systematic attention to the vicissitudes of the special relationship between therapist and patient is crucial to the conduct of the psychoanalytic psychotherapies. It constitutes both the subject and the object of analysis. Historically, two roles or stances for the therapist have been described in portraying the psychoanalytical psychotherapies: the primary stance with regard to the making of the transference relationship and, more recently, the secondary stance with regard to the making of a working or therapeutic alliance. Despite increasing acceptance of the latter into the therapeutic situation, these represent dual postures, which Greenson (1967) explicitly depicted as antithetical to each other, both in their essential purposes and in the actual requirements they make of the therapist.

The primary stance reflects Freud's (1911–1915) original recommendations (1) that the analyst be like a mirror to the patient, reflecting only what is shown to him or her by the patient and not bringing his or her own feelings (attitudes, values, personal likes) into play, and (2) that the analyst follow a posture of privation or rule of abstinence, that is, technical motives must unite with ethical ones in refraining from offering the patient the love that the patient will necessarily come to crave. These dictums have been taken to mean that two basic requirements are traditionally made of the analyst if he or she is to best accomplish the therapeutic task: (1) to continue to judiciously frustrate and avoid gratifying the wishes of the patient, and (2) to remain relatively removed and anonymous, a deliberately dispassionate observer and reflector of the patient's feelings. This also means that the therapeutic relationship is asymmetrical.

Conversely, within the same framework, the more recent concept of a working or therapeutic alliance reflects an alternatively non-regressive, rational, and more symmetrical relationship between patient and therapist. Although still in the service of analyzing transference and resistances, according to Chessick (1974), it means "that the therapist aims at forming a real and mature alliance with the conscious adult ego of the patient and encourages him to be a scientific partner in the exploration of his difficulties" (p. 72). The real object need of the patient, deliberately frustrated by the transference relationship, is satisfied by the therapeutic alliance.

Techniques and Methods

The major instruments of the prototypic dynamic approach are primarily verbal in nature. They rest in part on the proverbial "talking cure," and may be regarded as free association on the part of the patient and analysis of transference reactions and resistances on the part of the therapist. Analysis, the ongoing task of the therapist, is facilitated by four specific procedures: confrontation, clarification, interpretation, and working-through.

Free association early reflected the major verbal vehicle for communication of uncensored content from patient to therapist, to elicit the raw material on which analysis ultimately rests. This included the evocation of dreams, which Freud (1900–1901) regarded as "the royal road to a knowledge of the unconscious activities of the mind" (p. 608). Methodologically, the attempt to solicit free associations and dreams accounts for the most notorious material ingredient of the analytic method in classical analysis—the couch. Having the patient in a supine position unable to view the therapist and without extrinsic environmental intrusions is meant to create conditions of relative sensory deprivation that in turn serve to maximize the return of repressed memories.

With regard to the therapist's task and response to the verbal material elicited from the patient, the crux of the psychoanalytic method remains the analysis of transference, which comprises the major instrument of analysis as well as its major obstacle. The deliberate elucidation of transference reactions results in inevitable resistances to this endeavor, which must also be overcome as part of treatment. Methodologically, the reflective, ambiguous stance of the therapist in concert with the high frequency and regularity of contacts between patient and therapist are meant to encourage the regressive transference process and the intensity of feelings in the treatment situation.

Despite the endowment of the value of interpretation, the therapeutic path must be carefully paved in order for it to have its most beneficial effects. In this regard, the role of the techniques of confrontation, clarification, and working-through have been noted. *Confrontation* refers to having the patient discern or face the particular mental event to be investigated; *clarification* refers to placing the same event in sharp focus, separating important aspects from insignificant ones (both of these processes prepare for the actual interpretation); *interpretation* then goes beyond the manifest material by assigning an underlying meaning or cause to the event or phenomenon in question; finally, *working-through* refers to the repetitive, progressive, and elaborate explorations of the interpretations and resistances to them until the presented material has become fully integrated into the patient's understanding. This is perhaps the most time-consuming aspect of dynamic psychotherapy. Although the major thrust of treatment occurs within the therapist's office, working-through necessarily includes the tacit work done by the patient outside of the therapeutic hour.

In terms of comparisons with other forms of

treatment and their reputed curing powers, certain techniques or procedures are considered to be expressly anti-analytic, that is, blocking or lessening one's understanding or insight rather than facilitating it. Foremost in this regard are (perhaps ironically) abreaction, which may still be used but is not thought to directly bring insight; direct suggestion or advice, which is only useful to the extent that it is openly acknowledged and analyzed within the therapy setting; manipulation, allowable only to the extent that it can be brought into the analytic arena and does not occur without the ultimate knowledge of the patient; and the deliberate or conscious assumption of roles or attitudes that create an unanalyzable situation by their very nature.

Variations on the Dynamic Theme

The prototypical embodiment of the psychodynamic theme is, of course, classical psychoanalysis. The variations on the dynamic theme reflect overt and covert modifications of theoretical conceptualizations as well as methodological and technical applications in practice. These include attempts to partially or completely transcend the biological focus of Freud with more interpersonal, social, ethical, and cultural considerations (e.g., Adler, Horney, Sullivan, Fromm, Fromm-Reichmann, and

Meyer); to extend or enhance the ego with earlier or more adaptive endowments (e.g., Federn and Klein); to enlarge man's temporality with a focus on his primordial past (e.g., Jung), his present, and/or his future (e.g., Adler, Stekel, Rank, and Rado); to expand treatment procedures by altering the range and goals of treatment (e.g., Rank, Alexander, Deutsch, and Karpman); to develop guidelines for short-term psychotherapy (e.g., Sifneos, Davanloo, Strupp, and Luborsky), and even brief treatment of serious illness within the context of a single interview (e.g., Malan); to revise the role of the therapist's personality and relationship to the patient by making the therapist a more direct, flexible, and/or active participant (e.g., Adler, Sullivan, Rank, Alexander, Stekel, Ferenczi, and Rosen); and, at perhaps the opposing end of the analytic spectrum, to restore the psychophysical balance of man by focusing equally on the physical half of the psychophysical split (e.g., Rado and Masserman), and/or substituting an approach to therapeutic cure from the somatic side by trading the traditional mode of insight for a return to the earlier mode of catharsis, by means of the bodily release of conflictual tensions (e.g., Reich). More recently, conflict theory has been extended beyond an understanding of neuroses to that of pathological narcissism and borderline disorders (e.g.,

Masterson, Kernberg), while new dynamic thinking has ventured to deficits of the self as opposed to intrapsychic conflict, and the agent of insight has been replaced by that of empathy as a special attitude or context of the therapeutic encounter (Kohut).

THE BEHAVIORAL PARADIGM

> Whenever life becomes the object of science it suffers grief.
> Jacques Derrida, *The Ear of the Other*

Nature of Man and His Ills

The behavioral paradigm presumes that all behavior, both normal and abnormal, is a product of what man has learned or not learned. Neuroses or neurotic symptoms are construed as simple learned habits, involuntarily acquired, repeated, reinforced responses to specific stimuli in the environment. Indeed, Eysenck (1959) said that there is no neurosis underlying the symptom, but merely the symptom itself. Conversely, since external behaviors constitute the essence of the therapeutic problem, the therapeutic cure is simple: get rid of the symptom and you have eliminated neurosis.

Behavioral psychotherapy is an outgrowth of animal laboratory experiments with classically conditioned responses in which animals were observed to have habits that were like human phobias. Traditionally, behavioral psychotherapy also presumes that human neuroses have the same basic vicissitudes as those of the animal, in which anxiety (equated with fear) is regarded as its central manifestation (Wolpe 1969). Thus behavioral psychopathology is reducible to stimulus–response connections that can be isolated and altered in a piecemeal manner by inserting new associations. Viewed in this way, behavioral man is infinitely manipulable and therefore controllable by external events in the environment.

The prototype of orthodox behavior therapy is exemplified in Wolpe's reciprocal inhibition therapy, which is based on a classical conditioning model. Wolpe's main thesis is that neurotic symptoms are all essentially phobias based on the adverse learning of unrealistic fears. In behavioral theory this means that anxiety has been conditioned during highly disturbing or traumatic experiences.

Change or Curative Processes

For the behaviorist, all problems are construed as pedagogical in nature and therefore alterable only through direct teaching and learning of new behavioral associations, that is, stimulus–response connections. The patient must be taught new alternatives that must be repeated and practiced within as well as outside of the therapy situation. These alternative modes of functioning do not occur simply as a concomitant of cognitive or emotional understanding of one's problems; the patient must rehearse the new alternatives directly. Thus, in direct contrast to the psychodynamic schools, the behavioral approaches, according to Cautela (1970), tend to sustain the view that insight is not only unnecessary but usually hinders the treatment of deviant behavior. Wolpe's principle of reciprocal inhibition implies the rejection of catharsis as well. Wolpe sees abreaction (the symbolic re-evocation of a fearful past experience) as a special case in point, asserting that no permanent effects are achieved if unrelieved terror is the only emotional factor involved and is not counterposed by relaxation responses.

One implication of this view of the mode of therapeutic change is that change can presumably occur within a short period of time. Eysenck (1959) stated that all treatment of neurotic disorders is concerned with habits existing in the present; their historical development is largely irrelevant. Cautela (1970) went further to say that it is possible to have a situation in which symptoms have been removed with no knowledge at all of the etiology.

Although all behaviorists may be viewed as seeking change through direct conditioning, shaping, or training, Wolpe, in accordance with his classical conditioning model, sees all therapeutic learning or change (not just behavior therapy) as occurring within the reciprocal inhibition framework per se. Thus these therapies necessarily incorporate the substitution of relaxation for anxiety in the reduction or elimination of symptoms. However, more critically, the difference between behavior therapy and other therapeutic situations is that in the latter, counterconditioning of relaxation over anxiety occurs fortuitously or unsystematically, whereas in behavior therapy this process is overt, systematic, and under the direct control of the therapist.

Nature of the Therapeutic Relationship

The nature of the therapeutic relationship between therapist and patient in the behavioral therapies is, according to Hollander (1975), an essentially "educative, teacher–pupil relationship." In contrast to the psychodynamic transferential relationship, but comparable to the working or therapeutic alliance in certain respects, the behavioral relationship may be portrayed as a deliberately structured learning alliance; at its best, attention is drawn to the more current and presumably constructive aspects of the patient's personality in collaborating on the course of therapy.

Krasner (1962) depicted that behavior therapist as a learning technician or "social reinforcement machine." Although this phrase may apply to all therapies to greater or lesser degree, usually the behavioral therapist openly regards himself or herself as an instrument of direct behavioral influence or control, one who directly and systematically manipulates, shapes, and/or inserts his or her own values in the therapeutic encounter. In a comparable context, the therapist shapes his or her own behavior so as to be a social reinforcer for the patient. If the therapy does not proceed smoothly or effectively, the behavioral therapist revises the behavioral plan or schedule to better fit the treatment to the patient.

Behavioral therapy deliberately does not dwell on the therapist–patient relationship; at most, it does so secondarily, that is, according to the American Psychiatric Association's Task Force on Behavior Therapy, "only to the extent that this is seen to be important in securing the patient's cooperation with the therapist's treatment plan" (APA Task Force 1973, p. 27). Likewise, the behavioral therapist's use of warmth, acceptance, and any other relationship skills is common, but relegated to the realm of secondary "relationship skills" that are not crucial therapeutic requirements for desired change to occur in the patient (Hollander 1975).

Techniques and Methods

In Ehrenwald's (1966) words, the behavioral schools of psychotherapy actively relinquish "the methods of the couch" and replace them with "the methods of the classroom and the pulpit." The behavior therapist has at his or her disposal a large variety of conditioning, training, and other directive techniques. This repertoire may include any or all of the following: the more classical conditioning techniques of systematic desensitization combined with deep muscle relaxation, implosion, or assertiveness training; the operant techniques of positive or negative reinforcement; aversiveness training; shaping or modeling; and the more flexible directive techniques pertaining to the direct transmission of advice, guidance, persuasion, and exhortation. The latter methods more typically reflect the means by which behavior modification has been extended recently to the teaching or conditioning of cognitive behaviors or attitudes underlying specific behaviors, methods of philosophical indoctrination, or cognitive programming.

More generally, the behaviorist initially sets out to identify the patient's specific target behaviors or responses that need to be modified. These, in conjunction with the stimuli or environmental situations that give rise to the specific behaviors, constitute a behavioral formulation that may be regarded as the behaviorist's counterpart of the psychodynamic formulation. The behavioral formulation is used for the purpose of setting specific treatment goals, which are usually made explicit to the patient at the outset. The initial interview typically aims to specify what situations or factors contribute to the maintenance of the particular responses in question and on what occasions those responses in question are most likely elicited. On this basis the behavioral conditioning program can then begin.

Wolpe's classical reciprocal inhibition therapy, which has as its direct aim the reduction or inhibition of anxiety responses through the substitution of relaxation responses for anxiety, typically uses two basic techniques for the purpose of juxtaposing relaxation with anxiety. The first technique is progressive deep muscle relaxation training, and the second is systematic desensitization of anxiety through imagination. The patient is instructed to relax and then tense up for intervals of 10–15 seconds each; the patient repeats this maneuver using various different muscle groups or parts of the body, followed by breathing exercises. Then, after discussing with the patient which real-life situations arouse the phobic symptoms, the therapist incorporates each scene into an anxiety list; this list constitutes the basic therapeutic tool. (Each scene or situation is arranged hierarchically on the level of anxiety generated in the patient, with a ranking system of 1–10.) Starting with the weakest elicitor of anxiety in the hierarchy, the therapist asks the patient to imagine the anxious circumstance for a few minutes and then instructs the patient to concentrate on relaxing; this process is repeated until the patient can imagine the scene without feeling any anxiety. The therapist ascends the list item by item in the same manner. When this process is finished, the real-life situation that has created the phobia has lost its capacity to elicit anxiety.

A variation of this approach is, ironically, a direct reversal of this procedure. The therapist starts not with the bottom but with the top of the anxiety continuum; the patient is flooded with the strongest anxiety-eliciting stimulus situation of his or her imagination and keeps this in mind until the anxiety dissipates. Then, with successive repetitions of the same scene, the patient's anxiety progressively lessens until he/she is immune to anxiety in that situation. This basic technique is referred to as *implosion* (Stampfl's implosive therapy).

A cognitive variation of this approach is the technique of thought-stopping. In this variation, the patient puts into words the anxiety-producing situations instead of merely imagining them. As the patient speaks about himself or herself in these situations, the therapist suddenly interrupts the train of anxious verbalizations by shouting "Stop!" This procedure is repeated on successive occasions until the patient validates the fact that this overt suppression has indeed served to reduce the frequency of the anxiety-loaded thoughts. Ellis's (1975) rational-emotive therapy represents an elaboration of this cognitive approach on a larger and more varied scale.

The behavioral counterpart of the psychodynamic working-through is behavioral rehearsal within the confines of therapy, as well as assignments to be worked on outside of therapy; these are important parts of the total behavioral treatment. For example, the patient can be directly trained in certain social skills that may first be role-played or rehearsed within the course of therapy as well as explicitly instructed, tested in real-life situations, and reviewed in subsequent sessions.

A special instance of this method is assertiveness training, a technique of instructing and practice of interpersonal behaviors, which involves the relatively direct expression of one's positive and negative responses to others. Wolpe claimed that assertive responses constitute a major class of behaviors that could be used as an alternative to relaxation responses in the function of reciprocally inhibiting anxiety. Assertive training by means of behavior rehearsal, whether or not it is used as a technique for expressly countering anxiety, has been incorporated into a variety of schools that use the methods of the behavioral laboratory.

Variations on the Behavioral Theme

Three broad types of behavior therapies or behavior modification are considered under the umbrella of the behavioral theme (Mowrer 1966): one, based on the early classical Pavlovian paradigm, primarily uses systematic desensitization or extinction of anxiety techniques (e.g., Wolpe's reciprocal inhibition therapy); a second type, based on an operant Skinnerian paradigm, uses direct reinforcement by means of reward/punishment procedures (e.g., Ayllon and Azrin's token economy); and a third type, based on a human social learning paradigm, is contingent on direct modeling or shaping procedures (e.g., Bandura's modeling therapy). The latter type of therapy extends to a variety of new systems of directive psychotherapy that expressly aim at attitudinal or philosophical restructuring, using methods of the behaviorist's laboratory. Such so-called integrity therapies, although they share the fundamental learning or problem-solving stance, are usually more actively advisory and/or exhortative in their therapeutic techniques (e.g. Ellis's rational therapy, Glasser's reality therapy, and Sahakian's philosophic psychotherapy).

Another way of viewing the scope of these behavioral variations is through the evolution of their targets of change from external to internal alterations in man's learning. The earlier behavior therapeutic systems addressed overt behaviors and fears (e.g., Wolpe); the more recent systems are directed to covert values and beliefs (e.g., Ellis). For example, cognitive-behavioral therapy has emerged as a specific treatment for the targeted diagnosis of depression, as a way of directly altering depressogenic thoughts that are felt to lie at the heart of the disturbance. It aims to do so by recording and monitoring cognitions, correcting distorted themes with logic and experimental testing, and promoting self-control over distorted thinking patterns. A third broad behavioral approach ventures into the reaches of the most inaccessible and involuntary mental and physiological states and responses, such as heart rate, blood pressure, and brain waves (e.g., biofeedback).

THE EXPERIENTIAL PARADIGM

> If the patient is viewed as an object, the patient will tend to become an object.
> Carl Rogers, "Persons or Science? A Philosophical Question"

Nature of Man and His Ills

The experientialists criticize classical psychotherapy's overcommitment to the canons of science and its underplaying of man's ethical dimension, that is, his will, choices, and moral relation to others. Through psychotherapeutic practices and overemphasis on technique, man becomes impersonalized, compartmentalized, calculated, managed, and/or analyzed and thereby diminished instead of truly experienced by others or himself (Arieti 1975, Chessick 1974, Ford and Urban 1965, May et al. 1958). Experientialists also criticize the behavioral conceptualization.

The therapeutic process [is] essentially concerned with the experiential anguish of isolation and alienation. These experiences of

isolation, encapsulation, alienation derive
from social programming. . . . The central
problem cannot be understood exclusively at
the level of overt behavior, [but] must be understood as involving incongruence between
overt behavior and inner experience. Reinforcement learning theory is inadequate for
translating this central problem because it
doesn't include concepts representing human
experience. The behavioral therapy techniques associated with reinforcement learning
theory are potentially harmful because they
involve the very same programming approach
which induced these neurotic problems in the
first place. [Haigh 1965, p. 149]

The experiential conceptualization represents an increasingly emerging exaltation of
man in order to counter alienation, that is, the
fostering of the fullest exploration of the unique
and universal nature of man's self. It is expressly devoted to the self-transcendent quality
of human experience. This reaching out can
involve a transpersonal as well as intrapersonal dimension. According to Arendsen-Hein
(1974), the intrapersonal refers to an ego-
centered level, where the main concern is the
discovery of one's individuality, of one's emotional states and their representation in the
physical body; the transpersonal, on the other
hand, is spiritually oriented towards ultimate
reality, which means unity on the human, uni-

versal, or cosmic plane, in which one experiences a transcendence of ego boundaries into a universal consciousness.

The experientialist tends to view man as an inherently active, striving, self-affirming, and self-potentiating entity with almost limitless capacity for positive growth. The experiential therapies thus typically opt for growth, and not mere healing of illness. Their therapeutic goal is that of attaining maximal awareness or a higher state of consciousness, in which, according to May and colleagues (1958), "to be aware of one's world means at the same time to be designing it" (p. 60). Experientialists therefore direct themselves to such expansive dimensions as self-determination, creativity, and authenticity, and make use of a potpourri of methodologies that aspire to an ultimate integration of the mind, body, and more recently, soul of fragmented man.

The experiential stance historically reflects the incorporation of the basic philosophy of the European existentialist, with his or her concern for the essential issues of man's being or becoming; the methodology of the phenomenologist, who attempts to address data as given in order to tap their meaning, and to examine patients on their own terms without recourse to preconceived theoretical formulations of a causal or diagnostic nature; and, now more than ever, the religious teachings and techniques of the Eastern mystic, who presumes to bridge the mind–body split in seeking man's spiritual center. All focus on "man's most immediate experience . . . that to fully know *what* we are doing, to feel, to experience it all through our being, is much more important than to know *why*. For they hold, if we fully know the what, the why will come along by itself" (May et al. 1958, p. 83).

Pathology is regarded as the reduced expression of one's potential, the result of blocking and the loss of congruence with, or repressing of, one's internal self-experience. Both the psychodynamic and the experiential (essentially existential) themes depict the neurotic personality as suffering from repression and fragmentation. The dynamic view postulates repression of instinctual drives, especially sexual ones, while the experiential view construes repression as an ontological phenomenon, "the loss of a sense of being, together with the truncation of awareness and the locking up of potentialities which are the manifestation of this being" (May et al. 1958, p. 86).

Neurosis is a fundamental universal despair resulting from the individual's estrangement from himself and his society (or world). Comparably, anxiety, in marked contrast with the behavioral equation of anxiety with specific circumscribed fears, refers to "the anxiety of man facing the limits of his existence with the fullest implications . . . death, nothingness" (May et al. 1958, p. 118). Such anxiety manifests itself at every moment as man stands against the reaches of his own possibilities. Moreover, guilt accrues from the forfeiting of one's potential, for which the person alone is responsible. In Maslow's (1970) words, pathology is "human diminution" (instead of neurosis), "the loss or not-yet-actualization of human capacities and possibilities" (p. 124).

Change or Curative Processes

The experiential schools of psychotherapy trade intellectual cognition and insight for emotion and experience, forsaking the there and then of the distant past for the here and now of the immediate present. Experiencing is a process of feeling rather than knowing or verbalizing; occurs in the immediate present; is private and unobservable, but can be directly referred to by an individual as a felt datum in his own phenomenal field; acts as a guide to conceptualization; is implicitly meaningful, although it may not become explicitly so until later; and is a preconceptual organismic process. The many implicit meanings of a moment's experiencing are regarded not as already conceptual and then repressed; rather, they are considered in the awareness but as yet undifferentiated. In total, according to Gendlin

(1961), "therapeutic change occurs as a result of a process [of experiencing] in which implicit meanings are in awareness, and are intensely felt, directly referred to, and changed, without ever being put into words" (p. 239).

Therapeutic change through experiencing usually occurs by means of a real or congruent interpersonal relationship between the patient and the therapist. In the latter regard, May and associates (1958) have said: "Beyond all considerations of unconscious determinism—which are true in their partial context—the only thing that will grasp the patient, and in the long run make it possible [for him or her] to change, is to experience fully and deeply that [he or she] is doing precisely this to a real person . . . in this real moment" (p. 83).

One variation of this thesis, especially applicable to Rogers's client-centered therapy, reflects the underlying positive belief that every organism has an inborn tendency to develop its optimal capacities as long as it is placed in an optimal environment. Thus, according to Hoehn-Saric (1974), the patient is offered "an optimistic self-image; he understands that he is basically good and full of potentials. . . . Therefore, the therapist does not need to challenge or shape the patient, he has only to provide the warm and understanding milieu which will enable the patient to unfold his latent potentials" (p. 261). In addition, unlike transference, which is dependent on the revival of a former interpersonal relationship, experiential encounter works "through the very fact of its novelty" (May et al. 1958, p. 119). Through encounter the therapist serves as a catalyst in whose presence the patient comes to realize his own latent abilities for shaping his own self.

Nature of the Therapeutic Relationship

Although methods may vary, the real here-and-now therapeutic dialogue or mutual encounter between therapist and patient is the *sine qua non* of many of the experiential schools. It is, according to Ford and Urban (1972), "an emotionally arousing human relationship in which each person tries to communicate honestly with the other both verbally and nonverbally" (p. 470).

Rogers (1955) described the flavor of the therapeutic encounter as follows:

> I let myself go into the immediacy of the relationship where it is my total organism which takes over and is sensitive to the relationship, not simply my consciousness. I am not consciously responding in a playful or analytic way, but simply in an unreflective way to the other individual, my reaction being based (but not consciously) on my total organ-

ismic sensitivity to this other person. I live the relationship on this basis. [pp. 267–268]

These approaches to psychotherapy ideologically aspire to an egalitarian treatment model. The human alliance is not physician to patient or teacher to student but human being to human being. May and colleagues (1958) presented the following rationale: "The therapist is assumedly an expert; but, if he is not first of all a human being, his expertness will be irrelevant and quite possibly harmful" (p. 82). Thus the therapist must "enter the relationship not as a scientist, not as a physician who can accurately diagnose and cure, but as a person, entering into a personal relationship" (p. 267). Naturally, what one construes to fall within the domain of what is personal or real in a therapeutic relationship is open to interpretation.

Techniques and Methods

There is an assortment of schools of psychotherapy within the experiential theme that recoils at the idea of therapeutic technology. These schools, which are predominantly existential, renounce technique as part of their philosophy of understanding human existence. They feel that the chief block in the understanding of man in Western cultures has been an overemphasis on technique and a concomitant tendency to believe that understanding is a function of or related to technique. Rather, May and associates (1958) feel that "what distinguishes [forms of] existential therapy is not what the therapist would specifically do . . . but rather the *context* of his therapy" (p. 77). It is "not so much what the therapist says [or does] as what he *is* (Chessick 1974, p. 243). Indeed, in this regard the existential schools of psychotherapy have been criticized for their vagueness regarding technical matters in the conduct of psychotherapy.

Less harshly, the experiential schools aspire to flexibility or innovation in their actual methods as long as these methods are useful in the therapist's attempt to experience and share as far as possible the being of the patient. Here the aim or rationale of all techniques would be to enter the phenomenological world of the patient. In direct contrast to the view of the dynamic therapist, the experiential therapist does not concern himself or herself with the patient's past, the matter of diagnosis, the goal of insight, the issue of interpretation, or the subtle vicissitudes of transference and countertransference. Unlike the behavioral therapist, the experiential therapist expressly does not set goals for the patient and does not direct, confront, or otherwise impose his or her personality on the patient with directives in the

form of behavioral instructions or problem-
solving preferences. Moreover, techniques that
involve placing the therapist's judgments or
values above those of the patient are considered anathema to the requirements of uncon-
ditional acceptance of the patient and placing
the locus of control within the patient. It may
also be noted here that Rogerian methods as
well as others within the more classically existential framework retain a methodological
framework of essentially verbal interchange
between therapist and patient.

Although they share the same basic faith in
the therapeutic encounter and the emphasis
on feelings, other schools under the experiential umbrella are often less verbal. Such
schools (e.g., gestalt therapy), view verbaliza-
tion as overintellectualization that is part of the
patient's problem, that is, a manifestation of
defense against experiencing or feeling; they
discourage it as part of the therapeutic endeavor. These therapies attempt to accentuate
activity over reflection, emphasize doing
rather than saying, or, at the minimum, aim to
combine action with introspection. The goal of
experiencing oneself includes developing the
patient's awareness of bodily sensations, postures, tensions, and movements, with an emphasis on somatic processes. Awareness of
oneself as manifested in one's body is considered a highly mobilizing influence. The main

thrust of therapy is therefore to actively arouse, agitate, or excite the patient's experience of himself or herself, not simply let it happen.

Among the techniques for expressing one's self-experience in such schools is the combination of direct confrontation with dramatization, that is, role-playing and the living out of fantasy in the therapeutic situation. This means that under the direction (and often the creation) of the therapist, the patient is encouraged to play out parts of himself or herself, including physical parts, by inventing dialogues between them. Performing fantasies and dreams is typical, and is considered preferable to their mere verbal expression, interpretation, and cognitive comprehension. In variations of the somatic stance, body and sensory awareness may be fostered through methods of direct release of physical tension and even manipulations of the body to expel and/or intensify feeling.

In yet other attempts to unify mind, body, and even spirit, the immediate experience of oneself by focusing on one's spiritual dimension is sought. This is most often accomplished through the primary technique of meditation. The ultimate state of profound rest serves to transcend the world of the individual ego in that it is a higher reality or state of consciousness that the individual ego subserves. Major methods of will training and attention focused on a special word-sound or mantra, for example, serve to create an egoless or nonego-centered transcendent state.

Variations of the Experiential Theme

The therapeutic systems that have evolved under the experiential theme represent various approaches, each propelled by the immediate moment and geared toward the ultimate unity of man. These include: (1) a philosophic type, which reflects existential tenets as a basis for the conduct of psychotherapy and pivots on the here-and-now mutual dialogue or encounter while retaining essentially verbal techniques (e.g., Rogers's client-centered therapy and Frankl's logotherapy); (2) a somatic type, which reflects a subscription of nonverbal methods and aspiration to an integration of self by means of focusing attention on subjective body stimuli and sensory responses (e.g., Perls's gestalt therapy) and/or physical-motor modes of intense abreaction and emotional flooding in which the emphasis is on the bodily arousal and release of feeling (e.g., Lowen's bioenergetic analyses and Janov's primal scream therapy); and, finally, (3) a spiritual type, which emphasizes the final affirmation of self as a transcendental or transpersonal experience, extending man's experience of himself to higher cosmic levels of consciousness that ultimately aim to unify him with the universe. This is accomplished primarily by means of the renunciation of the individual ego in the establishment of an egoless state by meditation (i.e., relaxation plus focused attention). Here one reaches a state of profound rest (e.g., Transcendental Meditation), a spiritual synthesis that may be amplified by various techniques of self-discipline, will training, and the practice of disindentification (e.g., Assagioli's psychosynthesis).

Despite the respective repudiation by different detractors, the foregoing deconstruction of psychotherapy into three contrasting paradigms in no way is intended to add to their total negation. All schools need each other's adversarial presence, for the purpose of their own differentiating self-definition. In his chapter on deconstruction in context, Kojeve (1986) has suggested that "It does the man of the Fight no good to kill his adversary. . . . That is, he must leave him life and consciousness, and destroy only his autonomy" (p. 108). Indeed the art of deconstruction is always going to derive its philosophical fuel from others' assertions, while keeping their respective fires alive.

4

DECONSTRUCTION OF THE DUALISTIC DILEMMA: SPECIFICITY VERSUS NONSPECIFICITY OF CURE

As the discourses of theory continue to
proliferate and recombine into new
discourses, profound incompatibilities
and mutual contradictions emerge.
                              Howard Felperin,
                          Beyond Deconstruction

Beyond the belief in, or criticism of, the overarching paradigms of psychotherapy, or the
truth value of one or another particular system
of psychopathology and treatment, there have
been a variety of viewpoints regarding the
ways in which psychotherapy helps (and hope-
fully heals) the patient. In fact, trying to determine how psychotherapy "works" has been

one of the most vexing questions of the field. So divergent, and even antithetical, have been the attempted answers to this crucial query that they have resulted in a so-called "specificity versus nonspecificity" controversy. In its simplest descriptive and dichotomous form, this dualistic dilemma pertains to the question of whether unique (i.e., specific) or common (i.e., nonspecific) factors are responsible for therapeutic effectiveness.

On the one hand, the efficacy of each school of psychotherapy has typically been attributed by its respective founders and followers to features that distinguish their particular treatment or type of cure (Ellis 1962, Janov 1970, Lazarus 1976, May et al. 1958, Perls 1969, Wolpe 1958) . Similarly, certain special techniques or processes, such as analysis of transference, catharsis, systematic desensitization, and relaxation, have each been considered a crucial component of the therapeutic endeavor. Alternatively, especially in the light of the proliferation of diverse and often contrasting treatments of apparently equal efficacy, some investigators are placing less merit on individual modalities and their differences; they are seeking instead to locate underlying similarities or generic factors across treatments (Beutler 1983, Dewald 1976, Frank 1961, 1971, Frank and Frank 1991, Garfield 1980, Karasu 1977, 1979, Prince et al. 1968,

Strupp 1970, 1974, Tseng and McDermott 1975, White 1970). For example, Jerome Frank (1971), a pioneer in this search, has proposed a number of common elements that all therapies are presumed to share: an emotionally charged, confiding relationship; a therapeutic rationale that is accepted by patient and therapist; the provision of new information; a strengthening of the patient's expectation of help; new success experiences; and the arousal of one's emotions. To explain the universal therapeutic nature of these features, Frank's (1974, Frank and Frank 1991) "antidemoralization hypothesis" advances the thesis that it is the combating of demoralization which resides at psychotherapy's nonspecific core.

Further delving into the two horns of this dilemma reveals, however, that the terms *specificity* and *nonspecificity* have neither been used consistently nor been clearly defined. Klein and Rabkin (1984) have pointed out the need to distinguish between descriptive and theoretical meanings. They suggest that whether a particular facet of therapy is common or unique (descriptive meaning) is insufficient for a label of specificity, if by specific we mean that it has a special determining quality as a mechanism of amelioration (theoretical meaning). Review of the literature, in fact, reveals several conceptual connotations of these terms. This poses the possibility that the contributions of specific and nonspecific factors to therapeutic efficacy may not be mutually exclusive; both ideologically and clinically we could be dealing with a false dichotomy. It should also be noted that *nonspecific* does not mean elusive or scientifically inaccessible (although this is often implied by the term); rather, we should be able to delineate both sides of the specificity/nonspecificity coin. In order to do this, it is necessary to first deconstruct the components of the dualistic dilemma. The following thus elucidates three different opposing positions that can be carved from the core conceptualization into its constituent parts.

CONCEPT 1: SECTARIANISM VERSUS ECLECTICISM

One grows dependent on one's opponent.
Karl Jaspers, *General Psychopathology*

Contemporary counts of therapeutic schools and approaches reveal a plethora of presumably different types of psychotherapy. Implicitly or explicitly, these strategies have generally been exalted by their respective adherents, who suggest that they are not only different from, but more effective than, the others. The rationale here is that they are advantageous by virtue of their unique qualities, those that differentiate them from their competitors. For the most part, partisan allegiance to a single school or orientation, or in behalf of specific methods of treatment, continues to characterize current clinical theory, practice, and research. The originators and members of "new" systems of therapy may especially espouse this basic sectarian position in justification of their particular innovations, which often have been expressly designed to distinguish them from their predecessors and peers—whether they consider themselves neo-Freudian, behavioral, existential, gestaltist, primal, rational-emotive, or cognitive, to name a few (Herrick 1980).

A strictly separatist stance, however, has been the source of some criticism. From the point of view of the professional and his or her colleagues, it is thought to have produced pervasive polarization of the field (Marmor 1980). In addition, from a clinical vantage point, it has been regarded as ultimately antitherapeutic because it can preclude a more comprehensive vision of patient care (Lesse 1980). Moreover, singular claims of the overall advantage of one or another approach—still a highly controversial matter—remain essentially unproven. Scientific conclusions from a host of controlled outcome studies have never supported the exclusive effectiveness of a single school or modality for the myriad manifestations of mental distress (Smith et al. 1980, APA Commission on Psychotherapies 1982). Rather, the now classic conclusion from *Alice in Wonderland* regarding the results of a critical race, has become a psychotherapy research truth still applicable today, that "everyone has won and all must have prizes" (Luborsky et al. 1975).

Nonetheless, despite careful considerations that argue against specificity (qua sectarianism), the therapist's *belief* in his or her preferred mode of therapy may be an element in its success. Smith and colleagues (1980) have suggested that allegiance to a specific school or belief system appears necessary for the confidence and professional identity of the therapist; unenlightened eclecticism, by contrast, can foster confused therapists with marginal identities. They ironically concluded from their meta-analysis of the psychotherapies: "If anything, our findings warn against an eclecticism in practice that fails to differentiate into one type or other of psychotherapy" (p. 185). The need here is for a more enlightened eclecticism, such as the joint use of psychotherapy with pharmacotherapy in an additive model that addresses the somatic and intrapsychic aspects of psychopathology (Karasu 1982, 1990a,b), or the combined utilization of brief dynamic, cognitive and interpersonal therapies for different types or degrees of symptomatology within a multifaceted diagnosis such as depression (Karasu 1990). This means not merely applying an unplanned pluralistic approach, but also drawing upon the unique features of each respective modality to complement one another, in whole or in part.

CONCEPT 2: INDIVIDUALITY VERSUS UNIVERSALITY

> What treatment, by whom, is most
> effective for this individual, with that
> specific problem . . . ?
> G. L. Paul, "Strategy of Outcome Research
> in Psychotherapy"

A less exclusionary version of the specificity position has also been considered—not that a particular form of treatment surpasses the others unilaterally, but that a particular therapeutic agent is good for a particular problem. This is the basic "scientific" model, which is more often associated with the overall field of medicine (e.g., streptomycin for tuberculosis, digitalis for cardiac insufficiency). Credence for such a stance in psychotherapy is supported by those studies, however few, which reveal a comparable relationship between type of therapy and designated diagnosis. Recently, the advantage of modalities tailormade for a particular problem or type of patient, such as cognitive or interpersonal therapy for depressive disorders (Beck et al. 1979, Klerman et al. 1984, Rush et al. 1977), has been reported. Such a theoretical position has also been sociologically supported by cross-cultural findings, which reveal that treatment procedures accepted in one society or within the context of an indigenous belief system are not easily applicable to other social settings (Neki 1973, Wittkower and Warnes 1974). In efforts toward finer clinical delineation, this type of specificity concept has also provided the basis for specialized techniques of individual psychotherapy in the treatment of different patient populations—psychosomatic, borderline, dying, violent, and the like (Karasu and Bellak 1980).

Taken further, such a specificity thesis opts for the finest therapeutic tuning on behalf of the individual patient. In short, this specificity (qua individuality) position may be perfectly acceptable to the extent that each modality or technique, in all its uniqueness, is useful toward the amelioration of some form of mental suffering or especially suited to some patients but not others. Not only do therapeutic goals differ, but therapeutic effects can manifest themselves in a diversity of ways. At the most specific level, responsiveness from individual to individual may also vary from method to method, therapist to therapist, or time to time. However, the field of psychotherapy today is far from finding the best match of patients with particular methods, types of therapy, or styles of therapists. It has yet to discover Paul's (1967) ideal specificity of therapeutic effects, as queried above.

Simultaneously, the opposite side of this coin posits that therapeutic effectiveness really resides at its common core. In fact, in their comprehensive analysis of the benefits of psychotherapy, Smith and colleagues (1980) concluded, "The weight of the evidence that now rests in the balance so greatly favors the general factors interpretation of therapeutic efficacy that it can no longer be ignored" (p. 186). Thus, above and beyond (or in addition to) the specific features of major modalities that technically differentiate them from one another, a number of universal conditions of therapeutic change that unite all forms of treatment have been hypothesized (Beutler 1983, Dewald 1976, Frank 1961, 1971, Frank and Frank 1991, Garfield 1980, Karasu 1977, Prince et al. 1968, Strupp 1970, 1974, Tseng and McDermott 1975, White 1970).

Aside from equivocal research findings from extensive comparison studies of outcome (Luborsky et al. 1975, Smith et al. 1980), other lines of support have been cited for a universality thesis. These include cross-cultural, historical, and religious examinations of the recurrent nature of healing agents, particularly the placebogenic roles of suggestibility, persuasion, trust, and hope, in changing or curing patients throughout the ages (Frank and Frank 1991, Shapiro and Morris 1978); the paucity of proof that special technical skill, type of training, theoretical orientation, or professional discipline is significantly related to therapeutic results (Henry et al. 1973, Hogan 1979); and controlled studies of some commonly shared ingredients of successful outcome (Frank et al. 1978).

However, further exploration of this nonspecificity (qua universality) position reveals that the actual specification of these nonspecific factors has varied from theorist to theorist. Moreover, such factors tend to reflect different and often overlapping levels of generality. In this regard, Goldfried (1982) has proffered that commonalities must be sought at a level of abstraction somewhere between theory and technique.

CONCEPT 3: TECHNIQUES
VERSUS RELATIONSHIP

O' chestnut tree, great-rooted blossomer,
Are you the leaf, the blossom or the hole?
O' body swayed to music, a brightened glance,
how can we know the dancer from the dance?
      William Butler Yeats, "Among School Children"

The specificity versus nonspecificity dilemma has also manifested itself in a third usage of the terms—*techniques* as synonymous with specificity and *relationship* as synonymous with nonspecificity. This particular application has been the thrust of theoretical and experimental work by Strupp (1970, 1974, 1975) and Strupp and Hadley (1979). Conceptually it goes beyond the former meanings to suggest that the therapist–patient relationship is *the* supraordinate therapeutic influence that transcends particular techniques. In their research study of this thesis, Strupp and Hadley (1979) ultimately attributed the positive changes experienced by patients to the "healing effects of a benign human relationship" (p. 1135). At the same time, although the techniques of professional therapists did not seem to give rise to measurably superior treatment effects, specialized skills appeared to potentiate the natural healing processes of the relationship. In short, both the human and strategic aspects were important in effecting therapeutic change.

The above deconstruction of the dualistic dilemma does not presume to resolve the specificity versus nonspecificity controversy, but to perpetuate it as part of an exploratory process that resists resolution. It uses different manifestations of the dilemma, however antithetical their presumed postulates, to further elucidate the nonoperational nature of psychotherapy. Moreover, any such relative resolution shall undoubtedly pass through the portals of the scientific process, from which new problems and controversies are wrought and whose procedural tenets themselves need to be deconstructed.

5

DECONSTRUCTION OF THE SCIENTIFIC SCHEMA: PROBLEMS OF PSYCHOTHERAPY RESEARCH

> . . . the finished product of research
> disguises the nature of the work that
> produced it.
> > Thomas Kuhn, *The Essential Tension*

The bottom line questions of the efficacy of psychotherapy—when, for whom, and to what extent it produces therapeutic effects, indeed *if* it is effective, and even *what* it is—continue to be unsettled matters for the research scientist. The perennial problems of psychotherapy research methodology suggest that not only must the therapy itself be deconstructed, but also the scientific schema that is utilized to investigate it. We are limited not only by the boundaries of the treatment modality and the particular therapist, but by the constraints of "hard" science that are imposed upon the human ("soft") scientist. Indeed, in both scientific and nonscientific endeavors, it is believed that "what we assert is not so much its truth but rather just our knowledge of it" (Hegel 1986, p. 94).

RESEARCH DESIGN
AND SAMPLE SELECTION

> My relation . . . is not one of cognition, but of recognition, and this recognition ruins in me the power of knowing.
>
> Maurice Blanchot,
> *The Space of Literature*

Since psychotherapy research begins with the characteristics of patients and therapists as well as the characteristics of the therapy provided, the necessity for precise definitions and descriptions of these various elements that enter into the process of psychotherapy is evident. Therapist and therapy variables cannot be completely separated, and specified therapist variables are always in danger of being confounded with other uncontrolled variables, including the therapist's idiosyncratic inter-

pretation of treatment techniques. Neverthe-
less, it is incumbent upon any researcher to
characterize his or her sample of therapists
with the greatest possible accuracy in terms of
theoretical orientation, training, and experience, as well as in terms of the specific
methods and techniques used by them to
achieve their goals.

Once the patients, the therapists, and the
therapy under investigation have been described, it is then necessary to specify what
control or comparison groups are appropriate
for ruling out plausible alternative hypotheses
to account for experimental findings. There are
pros and cons in the use of untreated controls,
dropout and waiting-list controls, attention/
placebo controls, alternative treatment controls, crossover controls, and patients-as-their-
own controls. There is no single approach that
would be appropriate for the testing of all
hypotheses, and what type is best in any given
situation will be determined by both theoretical and empirical considerations. In fact, there
are at least five general ways of selecting and
assigning individuals to treatment and control
groups: random sampling, stratified random
sampling, cluster sampling, matching of pairs
of subjects, and matching of group means,
each with its own advantages and limitations.
The best method of attaining equivalent
groups when a sufficiently large pool of pa-

tients is available is through the use of randomization techniques. This method of assignment assumes that, in the long run, all significant variables will be equally distributed among the groups so that any differences found at the end of the study can be attributed, within statistically definable probability limits, to treatment effects rather than to extraneous patient or other variables.

Moreover, research designs for investigating the effectiveness of a particular mode of psychotherapy, or for studying the comparative efficacy of two or more therapeutic modalities, may geometrically increase the many dimensions involved. These include levels of inference permitted, time period under consideration, type of sampling procedures used, number of variables considered, and number of levels of each variable. One may thus conceptualize research design as existing on five different and increasingly complex levels. The five design levels are: the one-shot case study (Level I); the one-group pretest/posttest design (Level II); the extended baseline A–B design (Level III), which also includes the single case, $N = 1$ type design; the pretest/posttest control group design (Level IV); and multivariate designs (Level V), which include factorial designs. At each succeeding level, control is increased, the possible confounding of variables is reduced, the number of alternative explanations to account for findings is reduced, and the investigator's confidence that results are due to the specified intervention is increased.

Nonetheless there are advantages and disadvantages of each type of design, and not all good research need be conducted at Level V. Because of the tremendous investment in terms of personnel, time, money, and number of patients required by Level V designs, investigations at a lower level should probably be conducted prior to the conduct of these more complex designs. Their use is more properly reserved for the investigations of the differential effects of treatments whose parameters are well specified and that are known to be effective for specific types of patients.

In addition to the above relatively standard research designs, there are advantages and limitations of other design strategies. *Constructive* and *dismantling* strategies refer, respectively, to the adding of components designed to enhance the effects of therapy and to the elimination of certain treatment components from treatment in order to determine how crucial they are for behavior change. These strategies are recommended when the investigator is still in the process of trying to understand what the effective components of his or her treatment are. The lack of consistency in the findings of studies using these various strategies implies the need for alternative models for the conduct of research in this area.

Another general issue in psychotherapy research is how best to study process—the *how* of therapeutic change. Process research may be divided into two broad areas: in vivo studies that focus on the naturally occurring events in actual therapy sessions, and analogue studies in which variables are systematically manipulated under controlled conditions outside the therapy setting. There are serious methodological problems in the coding of observations that are usually recorded via film and/or audiotape for in vivo studies. While reliability and validity of observations made during in vivo studies pose a problem, generalizability to "real-life" situations is often problematic for analogue findings. Therefore, controlled experimentation needs to be complemented by replication studies in naturalistic settings; ideally, research should be conducted over the whole range, from the virtually unmodified clinical setting to the most abstracted laboratory conditions.

The last general issue concerns the ethics of psychotherapy research. There are three areas in which ethical issues lead to pragmatic difficulties and pragmatic issues lead to ethical problems. The invasion of privacy for the purpose of collecting the objective data necessary to evaluate psychotherapy systematically is one such area. The long tradition in medicine of reporting clinical findings that may benefit others may serve as a rationale for this practice. A second area concerns the ethical issues involved in assigning patients with distressing problems to lines for evaluation of experimental treatments. The third area relates to the possible refusal to participate in a study or to the differential attrition that may result from our ethical responsibility to obtain informed consent. The last area relates to the researchers themselves, the seekers of the knowledge—who are they and why are they? As Kierkegaard (1941) has proffered, "knowledge has a relationship to the knower" (p. 175). More specifically, he rhetorically poses the following problem and its proposed resolution:

> For an objective reflection the truth becomes an object, something objective, and thought must be pointed away from the subject. For a subjective reflection the truth becomes a matter of appropriation, of inwardness, of subjectivity, and thought must probe more deeply into the subject and his subjectivity.
>
> But then what? Shall we be compelled to remain in this disjunction, or may we not here accept the offer of benevolent assistance from the principle of mediation, so that the truth becomes an identity of subject and object? [p.171]

METHODOLOGIES AND ASSESSMENT
OF CHANGE

Form, after all, generates content, and not
vice versa.
Howard Felperin, *Beyond Deconstruction*

Among the methodological issues concerned
with the assessment of change in psychotherapy are the reliability and validity of techniques
for measuring the changes, the measurement of
therapeutic outcome, issues related to follow-
up procedures, the measurement of cost-effec-
tiveness and cost-benefit, and statistical issues.

There are controversies over outcome criteria, for example, what type of measuring instruments to use, who or what is to be the
source of information upon which to base evaluation, and the generality or specificity of assessment. Research on the effectiveness of
psychotherapy would benefit from an expanded set of outcome criteria, and changes
should be evaluated in many dimensions ob-
tained from as many sources as possible. For
example, batteries of instruments may be used
to assess different types of psychotherapy, but
it is doubtful that a single core battery can be
appropriately applied to all cases. There are advantages and disadvantages to measures designed to elicit information from different
viewpoints (that is, the patient, the therapist,
independent clinical evaluators, and commu-

nity members). Although the collection of information from all these sources can be both time consuming and expensive, each vantage point provides a unique perspective and each has some degree of validity.

A discussion of issues related to follow-up, and particularly to long-term follow-up procedures, centers on two main questions: how long should patients be followed, and what is the ultimate criterion of the success of therapy? Systematic investigation of follow-up patterns at varying times after treatment is needed. Regarding the criteria for treatment success, it is increasingly apparent that efficacy of a therapy should be evaluated not only with regard to its immediate results (however striking), but with reference to its long-term effectiveness as well.

COST-EFFECTIVENESS AND COST-BENEFIT

As psychotherapy becomes more cost-effective, we still have to ask, At what cost?
T. Byram Karasu,
"New Frontiers in Psychotherapy"

The growing issue of economics further complicates the evaluation of psychotherapy. The already multifaceted research that has been designed to test therapeutic effectiveness no longer suffices; the variable of cost has been added. There is a variety of methods to assess the costs and benefits of psychotherapy and to compare results generated by different studies. They are extremely complex procedures and, in general, have not been used to directly study a comparison of different psychotherapy treatments. Rather, they have most often been applied when policy decisions about large-scale programs or projects are needed. Thus a major emphasis has been placed on difficulties associated with measuring psychotherapy's benefits in monetary terms, and the literature tends to be concerned, perhaps even preoccupied, primarily with the value of low-cost treatments. In all cases, the usefulness of such analyses hinges on the availability and quality of outcome data, and it appears that greater methodological sophistication is needed before these techniques are fully applicable for economic evaluation. For better or worse, both the rationale for and the actual implementation of such studies are almost exclusively financial; alas, too little attention is given to the human price paid.

STATISTICAL ISSUES AND STRATEGIES

Absorption in methodological
self-legitimation cannot but be
counterproductive in some degree
for any discipline. . . .
　Howard Felperin, *Beyond Deconstruction*

The major problem associated with a frequently used mathematical method to assess psychotherapy outcome—changes in pretreatment/posttreatment raw scores—is that there are likely to be important pretreatment differences between groups, and a simple comparison of raw change scores could reflect not only treatment effects but these groups' pretreatment differences as well. The use of analysis of convariance and the use of final adjustment status alone to reduce the effect of initial differences are limited in their usefulness. These and additional considerations have led to the recommendation of residual change scores, which represent the difference between actual outcome and that which could be predicted from initial scores. This approach reduces but does not totally eliminate initial group differences.

Another statistical issue concerns the distinction between interrater agreement and interrater reliability. The importance of presenting both types of data, where appropriate, has been emphasized, and various procedures that have been suggested for determining these parameters were described and evaluated. Recommendations have been made concerning what are considered to be the best measures to use for data having different types of characteristics and properties. In spite of advances that have been made in the development of statistical techniques, all existing coefficients provide somewhat ambiguous solutions.

An additional problem in the use of statistics concerns the issue of statistical versus clinical significance. The level at which an investigator is willing to declare findings significant says nothing about the relative magnitude or clinical importance of the effect that has been observed. Of equal importance is the fact that the units in which we measure our outcome variables are not only arbitrary, but also without absolute meaning. These and other considerations underline the need for a concept of magnitude, or effect size, that is sufficiently general to be useful in all situations where a variable under consideration is scaled or dichotomized, that is not dependent on sample size, that yields a number that is independent of the units used to measure that variable.

An issue closely related to that of effect size concerns statistical power analysis, which may be viewed as the formal study of the complex relations that exist among four parameters: sample size; the magnitude of the phenomenon in the population, or effect size; significance level criterion; and power, that is, the probability of correctly rejecting the null hypothesis. There are potentially four ways of investigating the interrelations among these parameters. However, the major practical application of power analysis has been to make rationally based decisions as to sample sizes in the planning of research. It has been cautioned that the utilization of very large samples can make even the most clinically trivial results statistically significant, and that a large N can never replace good planning, reliable and valid measures, random sampling procedures, and all the other factors.

Due to the rapid expansion of research dealing with the efficacy of psychotherapy over the past thirty years, investigators who have attempted to review segments of the literature have had to develop schemas for deciding on methodological grounds which studies to include in their reviews and also for deciding on how to combine the results of large numbers of investigations whose results are often conflicting. The first comprehensive attempt in this behalf, to categorize and review controlled outcome studies, was conducted by Meltzoff and Kornreich (1970), who reviewed 101 studies and divided them into *adequate* and *questionable* categories on the basis of five criteria. A second subdivision, based on results, was then made that divided them into *positive, null,* and *negative.*

Since then a number of investigators have attempted to develop more detailed methods and criteria for comparing the results of outcome studies.With the exception of the more recent meta-analysis approach, all have basically been variations on the "box-score" method developed by Luborsky and his colleagues (1975). The box-score method is essentially a way of evaluating, in terms of a number of criteria, the quality of a study, and comparing, in terms of outcome, studies using different modalities or techniques of treatment. Studies that have assessed the effect of a specific modality of treatment on a specific outcome variable are examined. Studies showing positive, negative, or no effects in either direction are simply tallied. If a majority of the studies fall into one of these three categories, that category is assumed to give the best estimate of the true effect of that particular mode of treatment. A number of criticisms of this approach were noted, including the fact that it provides no rational or statistical basis for combining results of different investigations and that it ignores considerations of sample size in the studies integrated.

Meta-analysis, as developed by Smith and colleagues (1980) attempts to overcome the deficiencies of past techniques. To be included in a meta-analysis, a study must have at least one therapy treatment group that is compared to an untreated or waiting-list control group or to a different therapy group. It also must survive a number of exclusionary criteria. For each study included, information is collected on a large number of characteristics. However, since the most important feature of an outcome is the magnitude of the effect of the therapy employed, it is effect size with which meta-analysis is primarily concerned. Effect size may be calculated on any outcome variable, and in many cases a study may yield more than one effect size. Thus the effect sizes of the separate studies that meet the inclusion criteria become the dependent variables, while the independent variables consist of the characteristics of the study.

Meta-analysis as a methodological and statistical approach for integrating and analyzing large numbers of psychotherapy outcome studies is impressive in that it enables the researcher to extract information that would not be available from analysis of the individual studies. The approach is, however, not without its critics. One major criticism concerns the fact that the psychotherapies, the patients, and the therapists included in the meta-analysis are not representative of psychotherapy as it is practiced in the real world. Therefore, generalizations from the data are limited. Also, it has been questioned whether or not the hundreds of small, often poorly controlled studies may somehow be added up to produce one overall conclusion. As Felperin (1985) has sceptically concluded, "methodological complexity . . .

has the self-defeating effect, if not the intention, of obscuring what ought to be liberating knowledge" (p. 54).

UNRESOLVED OUTCOME ISSUES

> When we wish to see an oak with its massive trunk and spreading branches and foliage, we are not content to be shown an acorn instead.
>
> G.W.F. Hegel,
> *Phenomenology of Spirit*

The lack of resolution in determining positive—or negative—outcomes is in part a product of the complicated and subtle nature of the psychotherapeutic process; operationalizing and scientifically schematizing such an endeavor is inherently reductionistic. For example, although a number of papers have proposed the possibility of deterioration effects due to psychotherapy, and anecdotes on this topic have been reported by clinicians, research data on the subject is very limited. In addition, the idea of negative effects is fraught with conceptual as well as research problems. The most extensive review of this literature comes to the conclusion that about 5 percent of patients in psychotherapy get worse.

Controversy still reigns over the question of whether certain types of therapy are more effective than other types for certain kinds of problems. What has also not been adequately studied is what aspects or elements of the multifaceted therapeutic interaction are relatively the most effective. Another question at issue is spontaneous remission, which may be high in certain conditions.

In addition, the comparability of therapies bearing the same generic labels has been challenged, and many investigators have noted that relatively little is known about the actual process of psychotherapy and about the degree of variation that exists in the way that it is carried out. Attempts are now being made to create manuals designed to provide guidelines for the therapist on the conduct of different modes of therapy. Such guidelines may be useful in controlled research settings, but are believed by many clinicians to be largely inappropriate to the operation of their day-to-day practices. Currently it is unclear whether this apparent conflict between the research demands of reproducibility and standardization will ever be reconciled with the clinicians' need for flexibility, creativity, and sensitivity to the uniqueness of their individual patients.

Among the important conclusions of the various reviews of psychotherapy outcome is the fact that better-controlled studies do not show that therapy is more (or less) effective than do the less well-controlled studies. The use of double-blind techniques also does not appear to change the conclusions reached about therapy's effectiveness as compared to open studies. The relative effectiveness of psychotherapy appears to depend, at least in part, on the type of outcome measure used.

On the basis of the above, the point made that the laboratory type of research applied to psychotherapy tends to be of very limited generality raises the question of whether the laboratory model is the best or most appropriate paradigm for carrying out psychotherapy research. Obviously it is difficult to say what a new paradigm for psychotherapy research should be, but one may identify several relatively unexplored alternatives that may be helpful.

First, it is evident that one cannot justify untreated control groups for longer than very brief periods. One approach that has been suggested for dealing with this problem is to provide all patients with therapy, but to omit some essential ingredient for the control or comparison group. This procedure has sometimes been called a component control comparison.

A second alternative is to use community controls on a much larger scale than has hitherto been done. This would involve community surveys to identify one or more patient populations such as depressed, anxious, or phobic individuals, and then to follow them over long periods of time, particularly if they do not seek formal psychiatric treatment. Such a procedure would establish reasonable base rates of spontaneous remission and deterioration against which the data of psychotherapy studies may be compared.

A third alternative is to use scaled comparison groups in which patients are exposed to different degrees of psychotherapeutic interventions. From such data it should be possible to *extrapolate* the results to the hypothetical limits of zero intervention. This procedure thus creates data for a hypothetical control condition that is not obtainable in a direct way in the real world.

We should also continue and expand analogue studies, and not neglect $N = 1$ descriptive studies. Such designs are a useful form of research for developing hypotheses and as a source of new ideas. Most of the many psychotherapies in current use did not result from experimental research; rather, they are the outcome of clinical observation, insight, wisdom, and serendipity.

CONCLUSIONS

> What is known remains inexact, what is mastered insecure.
>
> Martin Heidegger,
> *Poetry, Language, Thought*

At its methodological best, the result of knowledge is still dependent on the interpretation,
whether in terms of Nietzsche's perspectivism,
whereby knowledge has countless meanings,
or Kierkegaard's subjectivism, whereby no absolute objective truth is possible. Conse-
quently, either way there are not facts, only
interpretations. And perhaps there are no interpretations, only interpreters.

An implication of this conclusion concerns
the considerable and continuing need for careful, systematic research on the effects of psychotherapy for various conditions. The present
diagnostic system is not adequate for psychotherapy research. In addition to the necessity
for precisely establishing diagnoses for patient
populations, attention should be directed toward developing a psychotherapy-related no-
sology and evaluation system. This should
take account of factors such as patients' conflicts, deficits, defenses, coping styles, and mo-
tivation as well as interactive variables, such
as the nature of the relationship between patient and therapist.

The second implication concerns the way in
which psychotherapy is to be defined. For example, for purposes of research it is not pro-
ductive to define psychotherapy in terms of
simple labels that refer to widely varying concepts ranging from specific procedures to broad-
ranging global strategies. This may especially

be the case with regard to manuals describing specific tools and techniques, applicable to specific disorders. In other cases, it might be preferable to delineate the therapy in terms of goals, strategies, and the nature of the transference between patient and therapist, as well as in terms of more specific factors. For example, Kernberg (1982) considers the type of transference (erotic or narcissistic, primitive or mature) as the most telling diagnostic dimension of clinical practice. Further, there is a need to understand in precise ways what the essential ingredients of psychotherapy are and also to define more precisely the different (and overlapping) strategies of psychotherapy. However, this operational approach to the definition of the practice of psychotherapy must be flexible enough to permit the practitioner both spontaneity and necessary therapeutic improvisation.

The search for knowledge of psychotherapy thus presents two alternatives: within the context of objective reflection, the truth can become an object, and at worst an outer "thing"; in the realm of subjective reflection, the truth becomes an inner matter of appropriation, and at worst a personal distortion. The question is, how does one come to terms with the limitations—and potential—of this dichotomy?

Even if all the above issues could be adequately resolved, unequivocal conclusions

about causal connections between treatment
and outcome may never be possible in psychotherapy research. In actual practice, psychotherapy is a highly individual set of interactions
that take place between individuals over an often indeterminate period of time. It is an open-
ended, interactive feedback process in contrast
to the closed, one-way causation that is typical
of most laboratory research. Research has not
as yet been able, and may never be able, to fully
document these elaborate series of interactions.
However, our objective should not be the impossible one of seeking the ultimate truth—as
disappointing as it must be—but rather of cre-
ating a framework that can provide at least successive approximations to it with partial
answers. As Thomas Kuhn (1977) has suggested in his treatise on the "essential tension"
between philosophy and science, even "exem-
plary applications . . . represent only a fraction
of the considerations relevant to the decision
process" (p. 327).

6

RECONSTRUCTION:
FROM SEPARATE
SCHOOLS TO
UNIVERSAL
HEALING
PROCESSES

Rapprochement is fully worth the quite
special effort it requires.
Thomas Kuhn, *The Essential Tension*

In light of the separate schools, competing
paradigms, and oppositional specificity versus
nonspecificity controversy of psychotherapy,
this chapter will utilize their deconstructive
components to reconstructively examine the
prospects for synthesis. By drawing upon
healing processes throughout history, this transcendent framework attempts to identify universal processes of change or curative agents
that all psychotherapies appear to share. Moreover, a deconstructive dissection of their sepa-

rate strengths and limitations aims to maximize the potential for positive interaction with the others. In short, this reconstruction represents the prospects for *rapprochement*— the integrative and collective capacity of the psychotherapies to balance and complement one another in clinical practice.

AFFECTIVE EXPERIENCING

> Beneficial to [mental] illness . . . , in general, is anything which thoroughly agitates the spirit.
> 　　　　Aulus Cornelius Celsus (25 B.C.–50 A.D.)

Some form of strong emotional arousal was probably the primary tool in the psychotherapeutic cures of primitive man. Often seances were conducted in the presence of a select group of individuals (the psychotherapists of their day), and emotional excitement was induced through smoking, drinking, drugs, and rhythmic music. Such affectively charged situations facilitated patient regression and eased the confession of sins. This type of affective purging process was the prototype for the earliest known structured psychotherapeutic attempt to deal with man's problems.

The specific Freudian version of this was, of

course, the now classic *cathartic method,*
whereby abreaction occurred, with the emergence of repressed memories through the technique of free association. Behavior therapies
have also had their affective counterparts in
reproducing anxiety-evoking stimuli in imagination or in vivo—with or without the accom-
paniment of relaxation techniques for purposes
of systematic desensitization. Flooding and
implosion procedures, for example, recreate
high-intensity exposure to feared objects or situations, with the expectation that patients will
experience their anxiety as fully as possible
and, exhausted with fear and relief, will no
longer respond as they used to. Similarly, aver-
sion therapy, by presenting an unpleasant and
sometimes painful stimulus, at least temporarily disrupts emotional equilibrium as a precursor of change through reconditioning.

But by far the most extensive resurgence of
the therapeutic use of emotional arousal and
release occurs in the experiential approaches.
Reichian therapy, Lowenian bioenergetics,
and Rolfian structural integration aim to express the affect trapped in the body posture not
by analyzing defensive character armor, as
Reich originally did, but by physically manip-
ulating the muscles that underline it. Psycho-
drama enacts the expression of feelings
through dramatic improvisations, while unin-
terrupted lengthy marathon sessions seek

emotional access through the byproducts of physical exhaustion. Comparably, primal scream therapy and Morita therapy use prolonged isolation and sensory deprivation to lower resistance and break down cognitive defenses—the former expressed in a sobbing, screaming, seizure-like episode to recapture the pain of the primal past, the latter by activating anxiety and distress as a preparatory step toward the creation of a state of spiritual readiness for rediscovering the beauty of life. A basic rationale for such diverse methods is that they aim to facilitate therapeutic change by "producing excessive cortical excitation, emotional exhaustion, and states of reduced resistance or hypersuggestibility" (Kiev 1966).

Research studies by Frank and colleagues (1978) confirm emotional arousal as one of the major effective ingredients of successful psychotherapy. Hoehn-Saric's work (1978) indicates that following strong abreaction there occurs a period of exhaustion which produces heightened acceptance, that is, "the patient appears bewildered, dependent and eager to find a comforting solution from the therapist" (p. 104). Three experiments have shown that heightened arousal made patients more receptive to suggestion and therefore more willing to change attitudes than they were under low-arousal conditions. Arousal combined with cognitive confusion yielded even better results than arousal in patients with undisturbed cognitive functions. Hoehn-Saric suggested that heightened arousal under conditions of cognitive disorganization helped to "unfreeze" attitudes necessary for change. Thus, affective experiencing as a universal agent of change may be globally defined as arousing excitement and responsiveness to suggestion through the unfreezing and expression of feelings.

The major roles and functions of affective experiencing may thus be to set the emotional stage for receptivity to change, to ease the cathartic release of repressed material, and to facilitate patient accessibility by reducing resistance and breaking down defenses. In short, the patient, through the dislodging of persistent chronic attitudes, may be made more available to a new cognitive paradigm.

However, Hoehn-Saric's (1978) research results also reflect the finding (often observed clinically) that intense emotional arousal, however profound and necessary to set the stage for therapeutic change to occur, was short-lived, and repeated interventions were required for such change to be established into a more stable new position. This observation parallels Freud's earlier acknowledgment of the limitations of the cathartic method and his significant theoretical transition from release of repressed affects and traumatic memories to their systematic exploration and understanding, that is, from catharsis to insight as the ultimate aim of therapy (Greenson 1967). It is also consistent with the research conclusion that although heightened arousal under conditions of cognitive organization helps to unfreeze an attitude, it does not necessarily lead to a new solution unless it is followed by cognitive learning (Lieberman et al. 1973).

Perhaps a major role of affective experiencing is to emotionally prepare the patient for new cognitive input. Indeed, pure catharsis is considered most effective only in certain limited psychiatric conditions (Leo 1969). Moreover, peak experiences, which may offer attractive opportunities for rapid change, often do not carry over beyond the immediate encounter. Weiner (1974), who compared three therapy groups of differing duration, found that the curative value of catharsis appeared to diminish in the longest-term group.

Thus, some form of affective experiencing appears to be universally applicable, but perhaps most effective as a preliminary stage of treatment. Ideally, this means that it should be succeeded by, or combined with, other change agents that have complementary roles or functions, in order to maximize or prolong its therapeutic effectiveness.

COGNITIVE MASTERY

> The soul is cured by certain incantations
> and these incantations are beautiful
> reasons.
>
> Plato (427–347 B.C.)

All therapies, in some measure, provide the patient with "beautiful reasons," whether they offer the classical, well-timed interpretations of Freudian psychoanalysis or, as in Ellis's rational-emotive therapy, have the therapist "singalong" with the patient a litany of the patient's irrational false beliefs. Cognitive mastery thus refers to those aspects of treatment that use reason and meaning (conscious or unconscious) over affect as their primary therapeutic tools, and that attempt to achieve their effects through the acquisition and integration of new perceptions, thinking patterns, and/or self-awareness. A prototype of a cognitive agent of change is represented in the therapeutic application of insight, defined by Harper (1959) as "the process by which the meaning, significance, pattern or use of an experience becomes clear—or the understanding which results from this process" (p. 163).

Historically, as Ehrenwald (1966) has pointed out, primitive faith healing and the early stages of psychotherapy were in fact very much alike in that neither initially attempted to provide insight. But while faith healing continued only to maximize suggestion (essentially through affective experiences), Western psychotherapy became distinctive in departing from the primitive mode by moving into a second state—to correct problems by explaining them rationally. Prince (1972) has gone somewhat further long this line by suggesting that, although the foundation of all therapies is the phenomenon of therapeutic suggestibility, primitive therapies are based almost entirely on irrational "belief and dependency," whereas Western scientific therapies are more often founded on rational "insight and independence."

Although insight (through free association and interpretation) has been considered a *sine qua non* of the psychoanalytic process (Blum 1979), all psychotherapies provide opportunities for change through cognitive channels—by means of explanation, clarification, new information, or even attack on irrational and self-defeating beliefs. Behavior therapies, once considered the antithesis of an insight-oriented approach, have increasingly incorporated cognitive learning techniques into their repertoire. In fact, Parloff and colleagues (1978) suggested that the behavioral model of treatment has radically changed from that of conditioning to social learning and information-processing.

Wolpe's behavioral technique of thought stop-
ping, a cognitive variation of classical conditioning methods to extinguish anxiety, can be
considered an early example of this change in
approach. Ellis's rational-emotive therapy,
Glasser's reality therapy, and Beck's cognitive
therapy all share direct attempts to correct
stereotyped, biased, or self-defeating thinking
patterns and dysfunctional attitudes and values, while others, like Frankl's logotherapy
and Sahakian's philosophical therapy, are directed to the most profound cognitive reap-
praisals of life and its meaning. Nielsen (1980)
has pointed out that even the most actively
experiential therapies use cognitive techniques and that gestalt "experiments" can be
considered cognitively as a structured interpretation.

   Thus, cognitive mastery as a universal therapeutic agent may be defined as acquiring and
integrating new perceptions, thinking patterns, and/or self-awareness, whether this is
effected through interpretations, explanations,
practical information, or direct confrontation
of faulty thoughts and images. In contrast to
affective experiencing, it serves as a rational
component of treatment to inform, assess, and
organize change and to establish or restore ego
control. Despite their therapeutic utility in providing a new perspective, meaning, or way of
thinking, predominantly cognitive approaches

are not always sufficient as agents of change. Referring to insight, for example, Schonbar (1965) made the double-barreled observations that not every change is the result of insight and not every insight results in change. Ludwig (1966) further pointed out that "there is no necessary relationship between the truth and falseness of insight and therapeutic results" (p.313). More broadly, there is also the tendency to equate cognitive change with a purely intellectual or rational process that precludes emotional understanding, although this distinction is difficult to validate (Richfield 1963). The belief is that cognitive approaches alone may produce over-intellectualization of problems or be mechanically applied in a rote manner to fend off feelings. (In most analytic circles, it is not considered true insight unless both cognitive and emotional understandings are integrated.)

Moreover, in his research study on the subject, Appelbaum (1976) found that the most common therapeutic problem was increased awareness without resolution. Not only were some patients unable to withstand the anxiety and other disturbing feelings consequent to increased awareness (what Appelbaum referred to as the "dangerous edge of insight"), but many patients "need not only to see and experience conflicts but to adapt and resolve them." This is consistent with Ludwig's (1966) criteria for attaining lasting insight—that it must be judged by its personal and social consequences. In short, new thinking (or insight) that has been achieved in therapy must be worked through and incorporated into one's actions and behavior in everyday life; it must be transferred from the structured and safe confines of the therapist's office and put into active practice in the real world outside of treatment. Thus, cognitive mastery, like affective experiencing, needs to be complemented by other therapeutic agents of change. More specifically, while the affective experience may prepare the patient for cognitive learning, the latter requires gradual assimilation and behavioral application of new input if therapeutic effects are to endure.

BEHAVIORAL REGULATION

> To make anything a habit, do it; to not make it a habit, do not do it; to unmake a habit, do something else in place of it.
> Epictetus (60–110 A.D.)

Whether one subscribes to a concept of cure that seeks ego strength and self-understanding through the vehicle of insight or aims for authenticity through the spontaneous expression of emotion, the final criterion of therapeutic change eventually resides in behavior. Behavior modification approaches have directly sought behavioral change as an active goal, and ultimately learning to self-regulate or control one's habitual responses has become the thrust of their therapeutic efforts.

Yet, like affective experiencing and cognitive mastery, behavioral regulation has particular limitations as a therapeutic agent. For some this may reside in the major goal of symptomatic relief, which can be construed as superficial or short-lived. An additional constraint is that focusing too closely on manifest symptoms has potential for diminution of the individual by separating the whole person from his or her problematic behavior. Moreover, because the assets of behavioral approaches largely derive from their rapid and objective application without having to deal with the deeper (and often lengthier) issues of the patient's subjective feelings, they may be remiss in not sufficiently expanding self-awareness.

Nonetheless, behavioral regulation serves the therapeutic functions of offering practical and expedient mastery of specified problems, reinforcing learning through repetition and practice of new behaviors as well as providing tangible application of change. Methodologically, this has meant the use of an extensive repertoire of reinforcement and training techniques based on research in experimental animal and human social learning laboratories— from classical conditioning to explicit rewards and punishments to shaping and modeling methods in imagination and in vivo.

Indeed, behavioral regulation as a major change agent is no longer limited to the classical confines of a conditioning model, nor is it restricted to the immediate territory of the behavior therapies. Even psychoanalysis, which has been considered relatively weak as a model for behavioral change and whose therapists must ideologically refrain from direct suggestion or deliberate manipulation, is by no means exempt from the use of behavioral regulation, at least implicitly. Strupp (1977) has enunciated four major examples of behavioral management in psychotherapy that relate to how the therapist elicits free associations, satisfies (or fails to satisfy) infantile needs, and responds to symptoms or neurotic behavior patterns. He points out, for example, that confrontation with repressed affects "is accomplished through consistent and persistent work on the defenses . . . [which] may be seen as a form of behavior management" (p. 12).

Likewise, all therapies, albeit in less systematic and sometimes unintentional ways, use methods of behavioral reinforcement, feedback, and modeling (Beutler 1983, Sturm

1972). Dollard and Miller (1982) have noted how analytic interpretation influences behavior by labeling, defining a problem, providing permission, implying a course of action, aiding foresight, and the like. In fact, research has experimentally demonstrated that subtle cues can shape the responses of patients. Examination of actual excerpts of Rogers's so-called nondirective therapy confirmed that even incidental nods or "hmms" by the therapist positively reinforce client responses (Murray 1956, Truax 1966). On a more inaccessible level, unconscious identification with the therapist is considered an essential aspect of shaping and modeling the patient's behavior (Offenkrantz and Tobin 1974, Volkan 1982). In the final analysis, Bellak (1977) conjectured that all therapy may be a matter of learning. Thus, to the extent that learning, modifying, and controlling actions and behaviors have been used therapeutically, behavioral regulation in all its variations has constituted a universal agent of change.

In sum, deconstruction from separate schools or modalities across the ages to the present time reveals universal healing processes that have been applicable then and now—and are likely to reappear in yet different shapes in the future. Modern forms are not necessarily new, but are reminiscent of variations of earlier methods of change or cure. In the matters of deconstruction and reconstruction, then, the words of Maurice Blanchot (1982) on literature may be equally apt to the psychotherapies, "What is present is not contemporary . . . but represents itself henceforth always to return" (pp. 29–30).

EPILOGUE: THE END OF THEORY AND THE LAST THERAPIST

Finally "the thing" itself always escapes.
J. Claude Evans,
Strategies of Deconstruction

As an ongoing process towards transcendence of theory, it is necessary for there to occur not only the natural course of historical dissolution and change in ideology, but a concerted deconstruction of man's most trusted tenets. This means a systematic undoing, or breaking down, of the infrastructures upon which favored theories, in all their intensity, are founded. Only then can a true reconstruction occur that is not infinitely bound by the tenacity of ideological preferences of the past.

Indeed Lehman's (1991) exposition on the rise and fall of theory supports the notion that "every generation defines itself in opposition to the one before it, in metaphorical acts of patricide" (p. 73); in the evolution of psychotherapy, this is true of the generational sequence of successive symbolic deaths (in effect, attempted assassinations) of one's respective predecessors. Thus the analytic tradition has been continually challenged, revamped, and in part succeeded by the behavioral tradition, which in turn has been conceptually contradicted, undermined, and replaced by an experiential tradition, only to be comparably dismissed by its predecessors and peers. This continuous course of counterposition and collapse has predicted an endless undoing and redoing of the prior heritage from which each has (however ambivalently) sprung. As much as these theories have attributed to the understanding (or misunderstanding) of human behavior, they are also responsible for the gap between theory and practice. Thus such theories cannot be looked to as justification for therapeutic practices, nor is the converse the case—the practice of psychotherapy cannot exist to justify these theories. In short, if psychotherapy is to forge its future, it must *begin with* the end of theory.

Insofar as the above necessity may seem obvious, the question arises: Why hasn't such effort begun with rigor? Are we afraid of losing

our increasingly shaky ground? Perhaps we
are the recipients of Cushman's (1995) contemporary concern, as he cautions that
"Simply acknowledging that our most cherished beliefs and institutions are constructions, and not reality itself, that chaos lurks
just beneath our various constructions is potentially too disorienting for us to often toler-
ate" (p. 16). I believe that the recent recipients
of the longstanding legacy of psychotherapy
need not be assured that the end of theory will
be a dark or dire foreboding of their future.
Rather, the practitioner who is imprisoned by
his or her theories can be set free, thus newly
able to draw upon—and/or discard with dis-
cernment—whatever "texts" are available, or
better yet, can be created anew within a recon-
structive context.

In a recent comparable treatise, the end of
history has been posited, based on the notion
that all of the major historical issues had been
settled. Here the individual who had outlasted
the termination of history "could not say anything new, only repeat earlier forms of igno-
rance" (Fukayama 1992, p. 311). What is
critical, however, is that the end of history can
also lay the goundwork for a universal foundation that surpasses all of its successive events
and ideas. Just as Fukayama is concerned with
the long-term effects of rival ideologies, and
with the "final forms" that mark the "end

point of mankind's ideological evolution" (p. xi), so I am anticipating here the final fate of psychotherapy and the psychotherapist's ideological as well as practical endpoint—the so-called last therapist. Such a therapist is one who is able to cast off the theoretical pulls of the past and to fend off the excessive use of theories to shore up the self. The final surviving clinician is the one who shall endure all of the conceptual schisms and schemas that predated him. He does not need theory to buttress his very being.

Over the centuries, different cultures developed their deserved therapies, primarily reflecting their respective beliefs and myths that often competed with one another, producing a problematic series of potential contradictions. But, according to Fukayama (1992), "A 'problem' does not become a 'contradiction' unless it is so serious that it not only cannot be solved within the system, but corrodes the legitimacy of the system itself such that the latter collapses under its own weight" (p. 136). History proceeds, says Hegel (1956), through a continual process of conflict, wherein systems of thought collide and fall apart from their internal contradictions. They are then repeatedly replaced by less contradictory and therefore presumably higher systems, which give rise to new and different contradictions, the so-called dialectic. This dialectic will remain as an important component of the evolution of psychotherapy within its own system (which thus far has continued to corrode the legitimacy of the practice of psychotherapy). Such a dialectic of theories of mind has unwittingly generated an evolution in psychotherapy that is directionless, random, and opportunistic, instead of a transcendent course that is unequivocally and unidirectionally cumulative, continuously building upon itself.

Like the end of history, the end of theory (i.e., theories of mind) does not imply that all the major issues in psychotherapy have been settled. Rather, there would be no further significant progress in the development of underlying principles of psychotherapy that do not repeat, or reify, prior theories. Due to the often unconscious need to idealize the past (Lehman 1991), dogmatic battles may continue among various theories of mind, which thus would not have a transcendent effect toward a more coherent and intelligible process of psychotherapy. Instead such perpetuation would constitute a reminder and reinforcement of the ancient biblical saying of Ecclesiastes in The Old Testament: "The thing that hath been, is that which shall be; and that which is done is that which shall be done: and there is no new thing under the sun."

The fateful thesis here, however, is that theoretical schools in the present age have entered their final stage. The task they had served at the endpoint of their existence has the same purpose they served at the beginning. Just as they served to supply the "first therapist's" associative needs, they will continue to do so for the last therapist as well. Such supplies are the contemporary equivalents of religion and basic belief systems, or more personally, provide a mirror stage for the therapist's need for recognition, in a Hegelian sense. Hegel (1967) described the "first man" (not unlike Locke, Hobbes, or Rousseau's man in the state of nature) possessing man's fundamental attributes, especially the desire to be wanted and recognized by others. Thus, while psychotherapy theory may still be useful to enhance professional identity and bonding with one's peers, it shall no longer be needed for therapist self-definition.

According to de Fontenelle (1688, cited in Nisbet 1969), a good cultivated mind contains all the minds of preceding centuries; it is but a single identical mind, which has been developing and improving itself all the time. Likewise, ideally the last therapist's mind would contain all the wisdom of preceding generations of therapists. But I believe that there is a cap on the factual knowledge in psychotherapy derived from theories, in fact that there is a potential for a degenerative process wherein some earlier knowledge will be wiped out.

In a more pragmatic vein, the end of theory can be termed atheoretical—or better yet, transtheoretical—as a new broad grounding context for the future clinician. Thus the end of theory may serve the last therapist well, always knowing that even endpoints are not fixed states; if deconstructed, they may even become new beginnings whereby, as Jaspers (1963) has proffered, a final "terra firma" is never reached. And the last therapist will dwell in that place which uncomfortably distances her- or himself from the primacy of theory.

REFERENCES

Adler, C. (1986). Psychotherapy of the narcissistic disorder patient. *American Journal of Psychiatry* 143:430–436.

APA Commission on Psychotherapies (1982). *Psychotherapy Research: Methodological and Efficacy Issues.* Washington, DC: American Psychiatric Association.

APA Task Force (1973). *Report 5: Behavior Therapy in Psychiatry.* Washington, DC: American Psychiatric Association.

Appelbaum, S. A. (1976). The dangerous edge of insight. *Psychotherapy: Theory, Research and Practice* 13:202–206.

Arendsen-Hein, G. W. (1974). Psychotherapy and the spiritual dimension of man. *Psychotherapy and Psychosomatics* 24:290–297.

Arieti, S. (1975). Psychiatric controversy: man's ethical dimension. *American Journal of Psychiatry* 132:39–42.

Ayllon, T., and Azrin, N. H. (1965). *The Token Economy.* New York: Appleton-Century-Crofts.

Bandura, A. (1969). *Principles of Behavior Modification.* New York: Holt, Rinehart and Winston.

Beck, A. T., Rush, A. J., Shaw, B. F., et al. (1979). *Cognitive Therapy of Depression.* New York: Guilford.

Bellak, L. (1977). Once over: what is psychotherapy? (editorial). *Journal of Nervous and Mental Disease* 165:295–299.

Beutler, L. (1983). *Eclectic Psychotherapy: A Systematic Approach.* New York: Pergamon.

Blanchot, M. (1982). *The Space of Literature,* trans. A. Smock. Lincoln, NE: University of Nebraska Press.

Blum, H. (1979). The curative and creative aspects of insight. *Journal of the American Psychoanalytic Association* 27 (Suppl.): 41–69.

Bromberg, W. (1959). *The Mind of Man.* New York: Harper and Row.

Cautela, J. (1970). Behavior therapy. In *Four Psychotherapies,* ed. L. Herscher, pp. 85–124. New York: Appleton-Century-Crofts.

Chessick, R. (1974). *The Technique and Practice of Intensive Psychotherapy.* New York: Jason Aronson.

Cushman, P. (1995). *Constructing the Self, Constructing America: A Cultural History of Psychotherapy.* New York: Addison-Wesley.

Derrida, J. (1967). *L'Ecriture et la Difference.* Paris: Editions de Seuil.

_____ (1985). *The Ear of the Other: Otobiography, Transference, Translation,* trans. P. Kamut. New York: Schocken.

Dewald, P. (1976). Toward a general concept of the therapeutic process. *International Journal of Psychoanalytic Psychotherapy* 5:283–299.

Dollard, J., and Miller, N. (1982). Techniques of therapeutic intervention. In *Converging Themes in Psychotherapy: Trends in Psychodynamic, Humanistic and Behavioral Practice,* ed. M. R. Goldfried, pp. 58–63. New York: Springer.

Ehrenwald, J. (1966). *Psychotherapy: Myth and Method, An Integrative Approach.* New York: Grune and Stratton.

Einstein, A. (1969). Autobiographical notes. In *Albert Einstein: Philosopher–Scientist,* ed. P. A. Schilpp. London: Cambridge University Press.

Ellis, A. (1962). *Reason and Emotion in Psychotherapy.* New York: Lyle Stuart.

_____ (1975). Rational-emotive therapy: a comprehensive approach to therapy. In *Issues and Approaches in the Psychological Therapies,* ed. D. Bannister, pp. 163–186. New York: Wiley.

Evans, J. C. (1991). *Strategies of Deconstruction: Derrida and the Myth of the Voice.* Minneapolis, MN: University of Minnesota Press.

Eysenck, H. J. (1959). Learning theory and behavior therapy. *Journal of Mental Science* 105:61–75.

Felperin, H. (1985). *Beyond Deconstruction: The*

Uses and Abuses of Literary Theory. New York: Oxford University Press.

Ford, D., and Urban, H. (1965). *Systems of Psychotherapy: A Comparative Study.* New York: Wiley.

Frank, J. (1961). *Persuasion and Healing: A Comparative Study of Psychotherapy.* Baltimore, MD: Johns Hopkins University Press.

_____ (1971). Therapeutic factors in psychotherapy. *American Journal of Psychotherapy* 25:350–361.

_____ (1974). Common features of psychotherapies and their patients. *Psychotherapy and Psychosomatics* 24:368–371.

Frank, J. D., and Frank, J. B. (1991). *Persuasion and Healing: A Comparative Study of Psychotherapy. 3rd ed.* Baltimore, MD: Johns Hopkins University Press.

Frank, J. D., Hoehn-Saric, R., Imber, S. D., et al. (1978). *Effective Ingredients of Successful Psychotherapy.* New York: Brunner/Mazel.

Freud, S. (1900–1901). The psychology of the dream-processes. *Standard Edition* 5:509–621.

_____ (1905). Three essays on the theory of sexuality. *Standard Edition* 7:125–248.

_____ (1911–1915). Papers on technique. *Standard Edition* 12:85–171.

_____ (1916–1917). Introductory lectures on psychoanalysis. *Standard Edition* 16.

_____ (1933). New introductory lectures on psychoanalysis. *Standard Edition* 22:1–18.

Friedman, L. (1988). *The Anatomy of Psychother-*

apy. Hillsdale, NJ: Analytic Press.

Fukayama, F. (1992). *The End of History and the Last Man*. New York: Avon.

Garfield, S. (1980). *Psychotherapy: An Eclectic Approach*. New York: Wiley.

Gendlin, E. (1961). Experiencing: a variable in the process of therapeutic change. *American Journal of Psychotherapy* 15:232–245.

Glasser, W. (1965). *Reality Therapy: A New Approach to Psychiatry*. New York: Harper & Row.

Goldfried, M. R., ed. (1982). *Converging Themes in Psychotherapy: Trends in Psychodynamic, Humanistic, and Behavioral Practice*. New York: Springer.

Greenson, R. (1967). *The Technique and Practice of Psychoanalysis*, vol. 1. New York: International Universities Press.

Haigh, G. (1965). Learning theory and alienation. *Psychotherapy: Theory, Research and Practice* 2:147–150.

Harper, R. A. (1959). *Psychoanalysis and Psychotherapy: 36 Systems*. Englewood Cliffs, NJ: Prentice-Hall.

Hegel, G.W.F. (1956). *The Philosophy of History*, trans. J. Sibree. New York: Dover.

_____ (1967). *The Phenomenology of Mind*, trans. J. B. Baillie. New York: Harper & Row.

_____ (1986). Phenomenology of spirit. In *Deconstruction in Context*, ed. M. C. Taylor, pp. 67–97. Chicago, IL: University of Chicago Press.

Heidegger, M. (1986). The origin of the work of art.

In *Deconstruction in Context*, ed. M. C. Taylor, pp. 256–279. Chicago, IL: University of Chicago Press.

Henry, W. E., Sims, J. H., and Spray, S. L. (1973). *Public and Private Lives of Psychotherapists*. San Francisco, CA: Jossey-Bass.

Herrick, R. (1980). *The Psychotherapy Handbook*. New York: New American Library.

Hoehn-Saric, R. (1974). Transcendence and psychotherapy. *American Journal of Psychotherapy* 28:252–263.

_____ (1978). Emotional arousal, attitude change, and psychotherapy. In *Effective Ingredients of Successful Psychotherapy*, ed. J. D. Frank, R. Hoehn-Saric, S. D. Imber, et al., pp. 73–106. New York: Brunner/Mazel.

Hogan, D. B. (1979). *The Regulation of Psychotherapists*, vol. 1. Cambridge, MA: Ballinger.

Hollander, M. (1975). Behavior therapy approach. In *Three Psychotherapies: A Clinical Comparison*, ed. C. Loew, N. Grayson, and G. Loew, pp. 220–236. New York: Brunner/Mazel.

Hutchinson, E. D. (1950). Varieties of insight. In *A Study of Interpersonal Relations*, ed. P. Mullahy, pp. 56–77. New York: Hermitage.

Janov, A. (1970). *The Primal Scream: Primal Therapy, the Cure for Neurosis*. New York: Putnam.

Jaspers, K. (1963). *General Psychopathology*. Chicago, IL: University of Chicago Press.

Karasu, T. B. (1977). Psychotherapies: an overview. *American Journal of Psychiatry* 134:851–863.

Karasu, T. B. (1979). Toward unification of psychotherapies: a complementary model. *American Journal of Psychotherapy* 33:555–563.

_____ (1982). Psychotherapy and pharmacotherapy: towards an integrative model. *American Journal of Psychiatry* 139:1102–1113.

_____ (1989). New frontiers in psychotherapy. *Journal of Clinical Psychiatry* 50:46–52.

_____ (1990a). Toward a clinical model of psychotherapy for depression, I: systematic comparison of three psychotherapies. *American Journal of Psychiatry* 147:133–147.

_____ (1990b). Toward a clinical model of psychotherapy for depression, II: integrative and selective treatment approach. *American Journal of Psychiatry* 147:269–278.

Karasu, T. B., and Bellak, L., eds. (1980). *Specialized Techniques in Individual Psychotherapy.* New York: Brunner/Mazel.

Kernberg, O. (1982). The theory of psychoanalytic psychotherapy. In *Curative Factors in Dynamic Psychotherapy*, ed. S. Slipp, pp. 21–43. New York: McGraw-Hill.

Kierkegaard, S. (1941). *Concluding Unscientific Postscript*, trans. W. Lowrie. Princeton: Princeton University Press. (Reprinted in *Deconstruction in Context*, ed. M. C. Taylor, pp. 169–190. Chicago, IL: University of Chicago Press.)

Kiev, A. (1966). Prescientific psychiatry. In *American Handbook of Psychiatry*, 1st ed., vol. 3, ed. S. Arieti, pp. 166–179. New York: Basic Books.

Klein, D., and Rabkin, J. (1984). Specificity and

strategy in psychotherapy research and practice. In *Psychotherapy Research: Where Are We and Where Should We Go?*, ed. J. B. W. Williams and R. L. Spitzer, pp. 306–331. New York: Guilford.

Klerman, G. L., Weissman, M. M., Rounsaville, B. J., et al. (1984). *Interpersonal Psychotherapy of Depression*. New York: Basic Books.

Kojeve, A. (1986). Introduction to the reading of Hegel. In *Deconstruction in Context*, ed. M. C. Taylor, pp. 98–120. Chicago, IL: University of Chicago Press.

Krasner, L. (1962). The therapist as a social reinforcement machine. In *Research in Psychotherapy*, vol. 2, ed. H. Strupp and L. Luborsky, pp. 61–94. Washington, DC: American Psychological Association.

Kuhn, T. (1962). *The Structure of Scientific Revolutions*. Chicago, IL: University of Chicago Press.

——— (1977). *The Essential Tension: Scientific Studies in Scientific Tradition and Change*. Chicago, IL: University of Chicago Press.

Lazarus, A. A. (1976). *Multimodal Behavior Therapy*. New York: Springer.

Lehman, D. (1991). *Signs of the Times: Deconstruction and the Fall of Paul De Man*. New York: Poseidon.

Leo, J. (1969). Danger is found in some remedies. *The New York Times*, February 9, p. 92.

Lesse S. (1980). Sources of individual and group decompensation in our future society: a psychosocial projection. *American Journal of*

Psychotherapy 34:308–321.

Levenson, E. (1983). *The Ambiguity of Change.* New York: Basic Books.

Lieberman, M. A., Yalom, I. D., and Miles, M. B. (1973). *Encounter Groups: First Facts.* New York: Basic Books.

Luborsky, L., Singer, B., and Luborsky, L. (1975). Comparative studies of psychotherapies: Is it true that "everyone has won and all must have prizes?" *Archives of General Psychiatry* 32:995–1008.

Ludwig, A. M. (1966). The formal characteristics of therapeutic insight. *American Journal of Psychotherapy* 20:305–318.

Marmor, J. (1980). Recent trends in psychotherapy. *American Journal of Psychiatry* 137: 409–416.

Maslow, A. H. (1970). Neurosis as a failure of personal growth. In *Psychopathology Today: Experimentation, Theory and Research,* ed. W. S. Sahakian, pp. 122–130. Itasca, IL: Peacock.

May, R., Angel, E., and Ellenberger, H. (1958). *Existence: A New Dimension in Psychiatry and Psychology.* New York: Basic Books.

Meltzoff, J., and Kornreich, M. (1970). *Research in Psychotherapy.* New York: Atherton.

Menninger, K. (1955). *The Human Mind.* New York: Knopf.

Michels, R. (1988). *Psychoanalysts' theories.* Freud Memorial Lecture. University College of London, London, England, January 25.

Mowrer, O. H. (1966), The behavior therapies, with

special reference to modeling and imitation. *American Journal of Psychotherapy* 20: 439–461.

Murray, E. J. (1956). A content-analysis method for studying psychotherapy. *Psychological Monographs* 70.

Naftulin, D., Donnelly, F., and Wolkon, G. (1975). Four therapeutic approaches to the same patient. *American Journal of Psychotherapy* 29:66–71.

Neki, J. S. (1973). Guru-chela relationship: the possibility of a therapeutic paradigm. *American Journal of Orthopsychiatry* 43:755–766.

Nielsen, A. C. (1980). Gestalt and psychoanalytic therapies: structural analysis and rapprochement. *American Journal of Psychother*apy 34:534–544.

Nisbet, R. (1969). *Social Change and History.* Oxford: Oxford University Press.

Offenkrantz, W., and Tobin, A. (1974). Psychoanalytic psychotherapy. *Archives of General Psychiatry* 30:593–606.

Parloff, M. (1975). *Twenty-five years of research in psychotherapy.* Lecture given at Albert Einstein College of Medicine, Department of Psychiatry, New York, Oct 17.

Parloff, M. B., Waskow, I. E., and Wolfe, B. E. (1978). Research on therapist variables in relation to process and outcome. In *Handbook of Psychotherapy and Behavior Change: An Empirical Analysis,* 2nd ed., ed. S. L. Garfield and A. E. Bergin, pp. 233–282. New York:

Wiley.

Paul, G. L. (1967). Strategy of outcome research in psychotherapy. *Journal of Consulting Psychology* 31:109–119.

Perls, F. (1969). *Gestalt Therapy Verbatim.* Lafayette, CA: Real People Press.

Prince, R. (1972). Fundamental differences of psychoanalysis and faith healing. *International Journal of Psychiatry* 10:125–128.

Prince, R., Leighton, A. H., and May, R. (1968). The therapeutic process in cross-cultural perspective—a symposium. *American Journal of Psychiatry* 124:1171–1183.

Random House Collegiate Dictionary, rev. ed. (1984). New York: Random House.

Rangell, L. (1985). On the theory of theory in psychoanalysis and the relation of theory to psychoanalytic therapy. *Journal of the American Psychoanalytic Association* 33:59–92.

Richfield, J. (1963). An analysis of the concept of insight. In *Psychoanalytic Clinical Interpretation*, ed. L. P. Paul. New York: Free Press.

Rogers, C. R. (1955). Persons or science? A philosophical question. *American Psychologist* 10:267–278.

Rush, A. J., Beck, A. T., Kovacs, M., et al. (1977). Comparative efficacy of cognitive therapy and pharmacotherapy in the treatment of depressed outpatients. *Cognitive Therapy and Research* 1:17–37.

Rychlak, J. (1965). The motives to psychotherapy. *Psychotherapy: Theory, Research and Prac-*

tice 2:151–157.

———— (1969). Lockean vs Kantian theoretical models and the "cause" of therapeutic change. *Psychotherapy: Theory, Research and Practice* 6:214–222.

Sahakian, W. S. (1976). *Psychotherapy and Counseling: Techniques of Intervention*, 2nd edition. Chicago, IL: Rand McNally.

Schonbar, R. A. (1965). Interpretation and insight in psychotherapy. *Psychotherapy: Theory, Research and Practice* 2:78–83.

Shapiro, A. K., and Morris, L. A. (1978). The placebo effect in medical and psychological therapies. In *Handbook of Psychotherapy and Behavior Change: An Empirical Analysis*, 2nd ed., ed. S. L. Garfield and A. E. Bergin, pp. 369–410. New York: Wiley.

Smith, M. L., Glass, G. V., and Miller, T. I. (1980). *The Benefits of Psychotherapy*. Baltimore, MD: Johns Hopkins University Press.

Spence, D. (1982). *Narrative Truth and Historical Truth*. New York: Norton.

———— (1990). Theories of the mind: Science or literature? *Poetics Today* 11:329–347.

Stampfli, T. G., and Levis, D. J. (1967). Essentials of implosive therapy: a learning-theory-based psychodynamic behavioral therapy. *Journal of Abnormal Psychology* 72:496–503.

Stephens, M. (1994). Jacques Derrida. *New York Times Magazine*, January 23, pp. 22–25.

Strupp, H. (1970). Specific versus nonspecific factors in psychotherapy and the problem of control. *Archives of General Psychiatry* 23:

393–401.

_____ (1974). On the basic ingredients of psychotherapy. *Psychotherapy and Psychosomatics* 24:249–260.

_____ (1975). Psychoanalysis, "focal psychotherapy," and the nature of the therapeutic influence. *Archives of General Psychiatry* 32: 127–135.

_____ (1977). A reformulation of the dynamics of the therapist's contribution. In *Effective Psychotherapy: A Handbook of Research,* ed. A. S. Gurman and A. M. Razin, pp. 1–22. New York: Pergamon.

Strupp, H. H., and Hadley, S. W. (1979). Specific vs nonspecific factors in psychotherapy, *Archives of General Psychiatry* 36:1125–1136.

Sturm, E. I. (1972). A model for the delineation of the psychotherapeutic intervention. *Journal of Nervous and Mental Disease* 114:332–343.

Sundland, D. M. (1977). Theoretical orientations of psychotherapies. In *Effective Psychotherapy: A Handbook of Research,* ed. A. S. Gurman and A. M. Razin, pp. 189–219. New York: Pergamon.

Taylor, M. C. (1986). *Deconstruction in Context.* Chicago, IL: University of Chicago Press.

Truax, C. B. (1966). Reinforcement and nonreinforcement in Rogerian psychotherapy. *Journal of Abnormal Psychology* 71:1–9.

Tseng, W-S., and McDermott, J. F., Jr. (1975). Psychotherapy, historical roots, universal elements, and cultural variations. *American Journal of Psychiatry* 132:378–384.

Volkan, V. D. (1982). Identification and related psychic events: their appearance in therapy and their curative value. In *Curative Factors in Dynamic Psychotherapy*, ed. S. Slipp, pp. 153–176. New York: McGraw-Hill.

Webster's Ninth New Collegiate Dictionary. (1989). Springfield, MA: Merriam-Webster.

Weiner, M. F. (1974). Generic versus interpersonal insight. *International Journal of Group Psychotherapy* 24:230–237.

White, R. (1970). Five basic processes in psychotherapy. In *Psychopathology Today: Experimentation, Theory and Research*, ed. W. Sahakian, pp. 596–599. Itasca, IL: Peacock.

Wittkower, E. D., and Warnes, H. (1974). Cultural aspects of psychotherapy. *American Journal of Psychotherapy* 28:566–573.

Wolpe, J. (1958). *Psychotherapy by Reciprocal Inhibition.* Stanford, CA: Stanford University Press.

——— (1969). *The Practice of Behavior Therapy.* New York: Pergamon.

Wright, K. (1991). *Vision and Separation: Between Mother and Baby.* Northvale, NJ: Jason Aronson.

CREDITS

The author gratefully acknowledges permission to reprint material from the following sources:

INDEX

ABOUT THE AUTHOR

T. Byram Karasu, M.D., is Professor of Psychiatry at Albert Einstein College of Medicine. Dr. Karasu was Chairman of the APA's Commission on Psychiatric Therapies, Chairman of its Task Force on Treatments of Psychiatric Disorders, and Chairman of its Work Group on Major Depressive Disorder. Dr. Karasu is Editor-in-Chief of the *American Journal of Psychotherapy*, and is on the editorial board of the *American Journal of Psychiatry, Contemporary Psychiatry*, the *Journal of Clinical Psychiatry*, the *Journal of Integrative and Eclectic Psychotherapy*, the *Journal of Psychosomatics*, and the *Journal of Psychotherapy Practice and Research.* He is the editor or co-editor of nine books and the author or co-author of more than 100 papers.